GW00362616

The
Guided Way

By Lucy McCullen

A counsellor's work with young people, seeking
solutions together through listening and writing

October 2014

The
Guided Way

© Lucy McCullen 2014
lucy_mccullen@yahoo.ie

ISBN: 978-0-9930341-0-7

Edited by Derek West, NAPD.

© Artwork, Niamh O'Neill

Graphic Design and Layout by Ailish Murphy

All rights reserved. No part of this book may be copied, reproduced or transmitted in any way without the prior permission of the publishers.

Published jointly by Lucy McCullen & NAPD

The Author gratefully acknowledges the support and endorsement by the National Association of Principals and Deputy Principals (NAPD)
Website: www.napd.ie
Email: info@napd.ie
Address: Eblana Villas, Grand Canal Street Lower, Dublin 2.

National Association of Principals and Deputy Principals
Cumann Náisiúnta Príomhoidí agus Príomhoidí Tánaisteacha

Printed by Printout
Professional Design & Printing Services
www.printout.ie

Dedicated to all the students,
who took the first step
and allowed their voices to be heard.

iii

"We must be a balm to other people's wounds"

- Etty Hilysum

Lucy McCullen and her fellow Guidance Counsellors provide the early intervention initiatives that help reduce problems and minimize the personal, relational and social damage on young people and their families. By the age of 13 years, one in three people in Ireland is likely to have experienced some type of mental health issue. Misuse of alcohol and other substances, self-harm, suicide ideation, study- or relationship-related stress, family difficulties, worries about sexual orientation, abusive situations can be the backdrop to the lives of students. Given the complexity of the problems, the student and the school community are to a great extent reliant on the expertise of the Guidance Counsellor.

Lucy's approach, and the power of the student voice in writing and reflecting on their stories, offer hope that difficulties can be addressed and even, at times, surmounted. Her practical suggestions and contacts to support agencies should prove a valuable resource and reference for all involved in the care of students.

It is only in relatively recent times that mental health issues have been openly addressed within Irish Society. However, school communities have been only too aware of the issues for many years. Students and their parents have benefited from the counseling service available in schools. Lucy provides a window into the work. On reflecting on the students' stories in *The Guided Way* it is difficult not to be struck by the irony that the service is now effectively discretionary, due to the removal of ex-quota status of Guidance Counsellors in 2012.

I have no doubt that Lucy's experience will be of assistance to others. Her generosity in providing this resource to schools and NAPD's vision in backing the project are commendable. May readers be encouraged to continue to "be the balm to other people's wounds" in their schools.

Pat Kinsella

Former Principal

Foreword

A key and essential element of the work of the NAPD Welfare Committee is to assist with the development and expansion of resources for Principals and Deputy Principal and this publication offers practical support and expert advice that, I believe, will be hugely beneficial to all school leaders.

The author has shared her own extensive personal experiences and insights into the behaviour of teenagers and outlined various methodologies that she has successfully used in dealing with young people in crisis. I am confident that the stories and reflections included in the book will prove to be an extremely valuable resource for those charged with managing schools and that the issues covered are relevant and representative of the challenges being faced by young people in schools today.

In addition, the book provides:

- An immediate and practical guide to help school leaders to understand and to get an insight into appropriate approaches and responses to the issues confronting young people on a daily basis.

- Relevant and useful data that will facilitate schools in devising the necessary strategies to empower young people as they try to cope with the journey of life.

- Appropriate advice and guidance that will assist schools to be proactive in promoting policies and procedures that will be of benefit to young people in crisis.

- An opportunity for a professional dialogue among staff on the nature and variety of counselling in schools today.

- An insight and awareness of how to recognise possible indicators to an underlying problem.

- Immediate access to helplines, websites and support groups.

This book is very timely as it raises awareness within the whole school community about the nature and variety of counselling in our schools today. It is not written as a handbook for staff to take on the specialised role of the Guidance Counsellor but rather is an additional resource that will support a whole-school approach to pastoral care and counselling. The book provides a clear understanding of the specialist role of counselling and makes a convincing case as to why the former ex-quota status of guidance counsellors needs to be urgently restored so that the ever-increasing demand for personal and social counselling from students can be addressed.

Shay Bannon

Chair, NAPD Welfare Committee

DISCLAIMER

The reader is reminded that the content of this publication is based on the experience of the Author. The views and opinions contained within this booklet are those of the Author only and do not necessarily reflect the views and opinions of the National Association of Principals and Deputy Principals (NAPD). NAPD does not warrant the accuracy, completeness or adequacy of the information provided and contained within this publication.

The information contained within this publication does not constitute legal or professional advice. The information is of a general nature only and is therefore unable to take into account each student's individual objectives, circumstances or needs. It should not be used, relied upon, or treated as a substitute for specific professional advice or legislative guidance. NAPD recommends that professional advice be obtained where appropriate before making a decision in relation to the particular requirements or circumstances of the student and/ or the school.

This publication contains links to third party websites. These links have been provided solely for you to obtain further information about the matters discussed. NAPD and the Author have no control over the information on these websites, or the products or services on them, and therefore makes no representations regarding the accuracy or suitability of such information or services. You are advised to make your own enquiries in relation to third parties described in this publication. Our inclusion of any third party content, or a link to a third party website, is not an endorsement of that content or third party website.

Contents

Introduction

For twenty years I have worked as a Guidance Counsellor in a large and vibrant community college. During that time the students I worked with have contributed to the counselling process through the medium of creative writing, helping them to explore, express and manage real-life difficulties they were faced with. The act of writing is therapeutic. By putting pen to paper three results unfold:

1. The writer confronts and makes real his or her feelings;

2. Clarity emerges;

3. Through writing, possibilities for rewriting the present, and future, arise.

Writing acts as a reflection. Students who engage in writing - letter or diary or journal or poem - find it empowers them to speak honestly. It allows them to see where they are and offers an opportunity to make changes. New perspectives are uncovered and understanding takes place. With understanding and a renewed perspective, change and hope are more tangible.

Over the years my filing cabinet has silently held these stories, words, letters and poems. In the current climate, where so many answers are sought by so many people, I want to give a voice to these creative pieces in order to offer solace, hope and encouragement to others. This is an opportunity to go beyond the confines of my office and to offer support and advice to those looking for guidance.

This book is written from my own experience and the knowledge and insight I have gained into teenage behaviour. It is my own perspective of the counselling process, highlighting the methods I have found to be useful and successful when working with teenagers in crisis. There are other techniques and approaches, used by many Guidance Counsellors around the country, which are equally effective. This book aims to raise awareness of the myriad of challenges faced by the 21st century student. The more sensitive we are to these challenges the more effective we become as educators. This effectiveness allows for the student to thrive and to reach his, or her, potential. Those students who seek advice and counselling become more active 'citizens' of the school, and, hopefully, of the wider community. Through awareness, schools become more holistic and complete. Learning, educating, teaching and leading all occur in a context. One of the objectives of counselling is to support this environment: to promote the aspiration, and the reality, that in the community of school the person 'suffering' will be listened to and helped. Good counsel is a key thread, combined with clear policies, awareness and practices, that forms a holistic and progressive school.

My Role as a Guidance Counsellor:

Every community has its specialists. Those who are skilled in any given field are approached and utilized for their expertise. However, the Guidance Counsellor, as a specialist, is part of a team devoted to delivering pastoral attention and responding to the needs of the individual in the community. This book therefore, should be used, and seen, as an opportunity to highlight the crucial importance of maintaining counselling at the centre of a school's endeavours. It is a confidential, available and free service and one that can only be provided by trained professionals.

As a Guidance Counsellor my sole objective is the welfare of the student. My role is not to change young people, but to equip them to live their lives to the full. I do not impose opinion or judgement, but rather, re-engagement with life. My aim has always been to facilitate students through listening and to provide them with a safe environment in which to explore their concerns. It has also been to provide the tools and strategies to empower their re-engagement with life in a healthier way and to cope with where the journey takes them.

Twenty Years On...

When I trained as a Guidance Counsellor I was young, enthusiastic and optimistic. The students I met, in the first few years, introduced me to new challenges and opened my eyes to different life situations. They became my teachers. With each new case, I acquired new skills and tried new approaches. As I learned my trade, I became more comfortable in my role. Each year brought new issues but a continuity of topics was evident. One of the things I concluded was that no two cases are ever the same. They are separated by the student's personality, reactions and background. Personalities determine how students respond and how I, as their counsellor intervene.

Today, I am still enthusiastic about the work I do. I am still optimistic, but I am wiser and older! The job remains a stressful one, hindered by the recent cuts to Guidance and the ever increasing demand in schools for personal and social counselling. Frustration is inevitable when faced with a shortage of mental health services, waiting lists and expectations on schools to be the channel for all interventions. The job is only possible with the support of Principals, Deputy Principals, teachers and parents. Thankfully, my experience has been that the participation of these partners has been a welcome and effective scaffold to the work done by Guidance Counsellors.

For Principals and Deputy Principals:

This book offers an insight into the lived reality for certain students. It offers targeted and appropriate approaches and responses to specific instances or crises. Its aim is to make school leaders more informed and therefore initiate and promote policies that support a deeper holistic climate. It is not intended to be used as a handbook of how to counsel but as a source of guidance and advice.

Guidance Counsellors liaise with all departments and personnel within the school. Principals and Deputy Principals are kept aware of individual cases, both formally and informally, as appropriate. This ensures that students have the unspoken, but active support of teachers and management. It allows both management and teachers to deal sensitively and appropriately with circumstances that arise in relation to the student, e.g. lack of academic progress, misbehaviour etc. As the Designated Liaison Person [DLP], the Principal is taken into a deeper confidence when the school has to act to protect a student's welfare. In these instances the Guidance Counsellor and Principal bring their professionalism and competencies together to act in the interests of the young person's welfare.

For Parents:

One of the primary aims of this book is to raise awareness amongst parents of the many issues that affect young people today. This readiness affords them the opportunity to be prepared. This book also strives to illustrate that they are not alone in coping. Both the school and the external agencies cited provide expertise and support for an individual in need.

For Teachers:

This book opens a window to the challenges faced by their students. This awareness empowers teachers. It is a reminder that no two students are the same. Informed teachers understand that ill-discipline and lack of academic progress is often rooted in a personal or social problem. While teachers can offer a variety of supports to students, that are worthwhile and helpful, each teacher must avail of the expertise provided by the Guidance Counselling Department, if positive progress is to be achieved.

For Students:

I hope students realise that they, too, are not alone. The experience and words of some of their peers should give them the courage to speak and reach for guidance. Teenagers are vulnerable and face many challenges. A heightened peer sensitivity towards those in need must be encouraged.

The Topics:

For this book, I have chosen a sample of twenty-five students from the 2,500 I have counselled over the past twenty years. The challenges faced by teenagers today, have not changed. However, the number of students for whom these issues arise has increased.

The Range of Issues Presented During a Counselling Appointment:

Transition to a New School
Bereavement of a Parent or Grandparent
Worries about a Parent's Illness
Pregnancy / Pregnancy Scares
Mum / Dad an Alcoholic
School Refusal
Self-Harm
Feelings of Depression
Suicidal Thoughts / Attempts
Exam-Stress
Panic Attacks
General Anxieties
Relationship Problems
Sexuality
Difficulties Forming and Maintaining Friendships
Sexual Abuse
Physical Abuse
Emotional Abuse
Separation of Parents
Eating Disorders
Obsessive Compulsive Disorders
Low Self-Esteem
Dealing with a Disability
Anger Management
Drug & Alcohol Abuse
Bullying
Involvement in the Gang Scene
Being a Non-National in the School

The nine topics I have chosen are the issues most frequently presented in counselling today and many are interrelated. The mental health issues associated with anxiety, stress and depression, have become the most prevalent.

In compiling the stories used in this book it became very evident that the writings are predominantly from female students. This is not to say that boys do not attend for counselling, but they are slower to put their thoughts into writing. I have found that boys between the ages of 12 and 14 find it very difficult to express themselves and often need a lot of encouragement to open up. A very positive fact is that of the numbers I now see for counselling (usually 10% of the school population), 50% are female and 50% are male.

For many of the students I met, the counselling process offered a place for them to talk and have their voices heard. It helped them to find positive ways of coping with difficulties, that life brought up for them. For most, it coincided with a new phase in their lives as they entered adulthood and had to learn to make decisions and take responsibility for their actions.

The Practicalities of Counselling in Second Level Schools:

- Students are referred by year heads, teachers, friends, management or by self-referral.

- Appointments generally last for 40 minutes – although this has to be flexible to allow for emergencies, interruptions and distressed students.

- The appointments are usually held in the Guidance Counsellor's office.

- Students are made aware that what we discuss is confidential except in circumstances where the counsellor considers them to be a danger to themselves or others, or at risk from another.

- Further appointments are offered based on the level of support needed.

- Students may be referred to services outside the school if the Guidance Counsellor decides it is necessary.

Time Constraints:

Every day I meet students who present with a range of symptoms, fears and concerns. Usually the underlying issue is not immediately clear, but clouded by confusion and despair. It often takes a lot of time, patience and persistence to help the student work through their difficulties before a positive outcome is achieved. The job of a Guidance Counsellor has become more inhibited by time constraints and the reduction in one-to-one counselling hours.

There are always more students to meet and not enough time. Disruptions during appointments are common and often distressed students appear at the door and time must then be found to facilitate their needs.

Age-Appropriate Intervention:

All the approaches I use and the referrals I make are age-appropriate. What works well with a 13-year-old, will not necessarily work well with a 17-year-old. What works well with a girl, may not work well with a boy. Getting to know the student is key to knowing which approach to use.

Referral Procedures:

Referrals are made in the following instances:

1. In emergencies, where immediate professional help is needed and the student's welfare is of serious concern: e.g. GPs, Mental Health Services, HSE or the Gardaí;
2. When specialised expert intervention is required: e.g. Cognitive Behavioural Therapists, Psychologists, Counsellors trained in specific areas or Support Groups;
3. When long-term counselling would benefit the student;
4. During holidays when continued support is necessary.

'Getting Closure':

The phrase 'getting closure' is often associated with counselling. The client seeks to deal with problems and bring the issues to a conclusion. Unfortunately it is not usually that simple. It is always waiting in the background ready to reappear. Unresolved, and sometimes even resolved issues, can simply lie dormant for a number of years. The immediate crisis may be overcome through counselling. Often closure really means simply giving the client the tools to manage. The hope in counselling is that the obstacle becomes a part of their history rather than their future. The crisis remains part of their life story, but does not define them. It is a paragraph in their life narrative, rather than a final chapter.

The Follow Up:

As with any process, there are stages in counselling. The follow-up stage is important, not just for the student, but for the Guidance Counsellor. It allows reflection and learning take place. What worked well? Why did it not work? What improvement can be made? What is the next step? The relationship forged between student and counsellor is generally a long-term one, based, as it is, on trust and confidence. I have been fortunate that many of those I have worked with have stayed in touch and often return for advice or reassurance. In this way, the conversation and the rewriting continues.

Author's Note: Anonymized Personal Details:

All of the accounts that follow are true and honest reflections of difficult and traumatic events experienced by a generation of Irish teenagers and are written in their own words. Each student has given their written permission for their writing to be included in this book and each is aware that changes have been made in order to protect their identity.

All identifying details and certain family circumstances have been changed for each student account, but with respect for the integrity of their story and creative work.

Chapter 1
Addiction

Clematis
Attractive and enticing, yet the nature of the clematis is to entwine and strangle, to gain hold.

Addiction

Addiction exists in all groups in society, whether it is an addiction to cigarettes, drugs, alcohol or gambling. All schools have health-promotion policies, encouraging healthy eating and healthy lifestyles. Subjects, such as Social, Personal and Health Education (SPHE) and Religion, in particular, assist students in making informed decisions about their own welfare.

TV campaigns and commercials continually encourage us to eat properly and to respect our bodies. Yet addiction continues to be a growing problem.

Students continue to smoke, drink excessively and experiment frequently with drugs, despite knowing the dangers. *Why? Is it a phase of teenage life? Is it pressure from peers? Is it boredom? Is it that drugs are more available? Is it because they are unhappy?* I don't believe that there is any one reason but a combination of reasons. In recent times, I have seen a huge increase in the effects of alcohol abuse among teenagers, the introduction of heroin and cocaine into the lives of a small number of students and a decrease in the use of Ecstasy and smoking hash / weed.

For the purpose of this chapter I have chosen three cases to highlight how addiction affects so many people, not just the individual most directly concerned. It is a complex problem and usually requires specialist intervention, sensitivity and considerable time.

In all instances students should be referred to the Guidance Counsellor. Depending on the seriousness of the addiction, the following steps may then be taken:

1.   The Guidance Counsellor works with the student to reduce the addiction, change habits and address any underlying issues;

2.   The parents are informed and given assistance on how to offer support;

3.   The Guidance Counsellor refers the student to a GP, who may then make a referral to an addiction centre or addiction counsellor.

Possible Signs Of Addiction To Look Out For:

(Remember some of these signs are associated with normal changes in growth and development.)

Facial skin changes, spots and sores

Pale and tired appearance

Weight loss

Dilated pupils

Lethargy

Loss in concentration

Loss of interest in hobbies and school

Moody and aggressive

Money issues - selling off possessions or stealing

Introducing Emily... Aged 15...

Emily attended counselling because her brother Jack was addicted to alcohol and drugs. For this 15-year-old girl, it was devastating to watch him deteriorate before her eyes. She felt powerless, exhausted, angry and guilty. He always came home "off his head", aggressive, disruptive and argumentative. He had a drugs debt that had spiralled into thousands of euro. He got involved in fights and was found stealing prescription medication. He was in serious trouble. Like him, their home had become unstable, erratic and dysfunctional. Relationships became frayed and volatile. It was evident that her brother was rapidly deteriorating physically - he was under-weight and unco-ordinated. She was terrified that he would do himself harm. She watched him stagger and fall to the ground many times. She worried that, one day, he would fall down and he wouldn't get back up.

I'm scared in case something happens. I don't want to think later on that I could have done something. But I just don't know what to do. I have a terrible feeling that something bad is going to happen.

The Approach I Used...

Emily presented a situation in which everything felt totally outside of her control. Many people had tried to talk to Jack and to encourage him to seek help, but to no avail. Twice a week she came for counselling. It was a place for her to talk in confidence. She enjoyed writing and it was through the medium of creative writing that she could express her fears. I encouraged Emily to write a journal of poetry. In each session we discussed her poems and, in so doing, discussed her problems. They became her way of unburdening and unloading all the pain she was suffering. My role was to facilitate this process and to allow her the space and time to work through it. As the sessions continued the poems developed. Initially, she wrote using phrases of a similar negative tone:

In the shadow of darkness
Trapped here alone
I'm strangled with fear

All of this expressed the feeling that she was totally overwhelmed by her brother's addiction and consequent actions. As her counsellor there were many times I also felt overwhelmed, such was the grief and desperation in front of me. However, it is this connection that helps the counselling process to work. I knew I needed to concentrate on breaking up the confusion of emotions into manageable parts. When speaking with Emily I used language that was reassuring and encouraging, while always calm and considered. Gradually her thoughts became clearer and her words more determined. She cried less during appointments and she became more focused on controlling her own thoughts and feelings.

The following is a poem Emily wrote during the counselling process.

The Bright Star

All alone one lonely night
Stars sparkle out in the naked sky
But sorrow I wash down with me
Far beyond and past the light.

But suddenly I see my face
As I look deeper through
I stare and look at me
Not wanting to keep and see.

Quickly I wipe away
I see through that open door
But far away out into the distance
I see a fallen star.

Looking at this bright star fall
My heart sinks in pain
This star was once a sparkle
But a sparkle through my day.

Then, the star twinkles
Almost as if to whisper
Don't blow your twinkle away
But keep it safe and near.

During a stay in a treatment centre, Emily's brother, twenty-year-old Jack wrote the following poem, with remarkable clarity and precision. In his writings he portrays a high level of self-awareness despite his struggle with addictions.

A New Beginning

At the start it was all just fun,
Going out with friends is what we all done.
Having a drink at first was a laugh
But along came the drug scene and the fun didn't last.
Taking Es and speed seemed so much fun.
Up dancing all night to the sound of a beating drum
It's when the music stops and you start to come down
That you need something else to take away the frown.

So soon that frown turns to delight
As you get the foil and skin up a joint
But as the weeks go by you don't notice the changes
Except for the track marks left in certain places.

Then one morning you wake up sick and shaking
You think it's the flu but soon are mistaking
For there is a strange craving inside your head
That won't go away until it is fed.
And feed it you do and all seems well
But only for a few hours and its back to hell.
As time kicks on and problems pop up
What better way to deal with them
than to get up and go to your nearest dealer
And once again hand over more money for another problem healer.
Its only when people close to you and loved ones start to disappear
Not wanting to know you out of fear
Of what you have become-a slave to a drug which alters your mind
And helps to block out everything including space and time.

When all seems lost and you wish for all to end
There are two ways to go and one will mean the end.
The other is to stop and think about the life you have been living
And ask for help and start a new beginning.
Whether it's God or a friend who help you get there.
Don't be afraid because one day you too can share and help
Someone that is in the same boat
And step by step help others to stay afloat.

The Follow Up...

Unfortunately for Emily her biggest fear came true. Jack died not long after leaving the treatment centre. He was high on a concoction of drugs and alcohol when he fell and never got back up. It was a terrible blow to Emily and all her family. It was a tragic irony that Jack had moments of clarity and a desire for a 'new beginning', but the hold that his addiction had was too great. It is this harsh reality which conveys the profound power addiction has to destroy those within its grasp.

The counselling process was very beneficial for Emily. She had a place where she was listened to, encouraged and allowed to be herself. Through it she found calm in her otherwise chaotic world. When she came to me first it was due to her brother's addiction to drugs and alcohol; now she was faced with grieving for him. She continued to attend for counselling and to write poetry. Through both she experienced and understood the different stages of grief and how each one affected her. When she left the school she left with a set of skills to help her cope with further struggles.

Today, Emily works in a caring profession and continues to look after others. She is a wonderful role model for all who experience traumatic incidents and conquer them. I know she still struggles with the losses she has had. They are a part of her and will never leave her.

Introducing Susan... Aged 17...

Susan was a Leaving Certificate student who presented initially with the seemingly minor issue of a lack of motivation. As time went by and she developed a trust in me as her Guidance Counsellor, she revealed that she was struggling to cope with a childhood memory of being abused, that only surfaced as she found herself in relationships. This is often the case if a child has supressed a traumatic event from the past that they cannot cope with. She had turned to both alcohol and drugs to numb the painful feelings of hurt, guilt and anger. She was drinking heavily, not just at the weekends but on school days too. She was feeling down in herself and had lost all her confidence. She knew she needed help.

The Approach I Used...

For Susan, the addiction to alcohol and drugs was a symptom of a much deeper problem, that of being sexually abused as a young child. (Her family were aware of it and procedures had already been followed when she was in primary school.) The first step for me was to address the habitual drinking that was occurring every day. She had also developed a tremor in her hands that was quite noticeable. She had to take small steps to reform her way of life and gain control again.

Each week she was given the task of reducing the number of days when she was drinking. She had to keep a diary each day, which helped her see how her actions shaped her emotions. Over the course of six weeks she reduced her drinking to Saturday nights. I also arranged for her to get a job in the school shop, a small way of building her confidence and taking responsibility for herself. She had still a long way to go and deeper issues to come to terms with. But she was now, after six weeks, in a position to confront the deeper problem. Having excluded alcohol from her everyday life she was in a stronger position to deal with the cause of her unhappiness.

Susan's Story...

This is a letter Susan wrote to me before a counselling appointment.

Just thinking about everything, I can see that when things went wrong I took drugs. Then I got a fright and stopped. But then I go away and start drinking. I don't want to have an accident or something before it makes me realise how far it's gone, because at this stage I know myself, it's gone too far.
Bhí glincín sa ghrágán agam. (I have taken a drop)

I can't believe I'm after letting things go so far, but it's my own fault. I don't know. I just can't deal with things anymore and these things like my hands shaking or my legs shaking or seeing things in front of me that aren't there, are finally freaking me out!
Níl a thuilleadh le rá agam anois. (I have nothing more to say now)

After meeting with Susan for several weeks we spoke about getting help outside of school. Initially, she refused, as many students do. But she came round to the idea. I sat in on the first session with the counsellor to help "tell her story". She was very brave to take that first step. The relief of sharing her troubles was far greater than the fear of opening up to a stranger. She began to trust again and put faith in her own ability to use her own resources to fight the addiction.

Since I had referred Susan to another counsellor we finished the appointments in school and I continued to monitor her. This would be the normal procedure for two key reasons:

1.   It would cause confusion to the student to have two different counsellors who might have different methods of counselling;

2.   With the time constraints and numbers attending for counselling in schools there are always more students to meet.

As with any addiction, there were relapses. Susan continued to find herself tempted by alcohol to suppress the emotions brought up through the counselling process. It was a very tough time for her. She still doubted herself and was very confused. The Leaving Certificate is for all students both stressful and draining, but for a student like Susan, it was even more so.

Throughout her young life she lived with abuse and struggled to fight the demon of addiction. She got through the exams and went straight into work. She managed to maintain that job and has progressed within the company. If she had not taken the first step to attend for counselling she may have had a very different path into adulthood. When students move on, we often do not know how they get on afterwards. I did however receive a note of thanks from Susan some years later. In it she wrote:

I don't often remember what it was you said to me, but I remember how you made me feel.

Introducing Anna... Aged 17...

Anna's father had a gambling addiction. She knew it, her mother knew it and he probably knew it. But it was never spoken of, or addressed, in the home. His job provided the only income to cover the running costs of the house and everyday life. Initially, the stresses showed in small ways: amounts of money went missing, bills were not paid on time and money was not available for the little things. The difficulties escalated. Every evening after work he would leave the house and not return for several hours.

All the signs of a growing addiction were present:

He had become evasive;
He was dishonest;
He suffered mood swings;
His absences were more prolonged;
There was an evident anxiety associated with a variety of sporting events, e.g. horse-racing.

She was worried, not just about the financial burden, but the effect it was having on her mother who was becoming withdrawn and frequently upset. Her mother secured some part-time work, but still they seemed to be struggling. Anna herself searched for a job to help out. She was very angry at her father. He was never there for her or her mother. The emotional and financial burdens continued to impact. Her father had disengaged from normal family life as the addiction became more profound.

As time passed, and the situation became more intolerable, she tried talking to him, but it was no good because he refused to accept the premise that an addiction or problem existed.

Anna's Story...

This is the letter Anna wrote to her father expressing how his addiction made her feel. She did not give him the letter but it helped her to get her feelings out and on paper.

I wish you would just grow up and act like a husband and a dad. Stop gambling which I know you are doing and start supporting your family financially and emotionally. It's as if I grew up without a dad. You were never there for me and I hate you for that and you think you would start making it up to me now but no, you act as if I'm not even there and don't even make any effort to make conversation with me not to mind actually spending time with me.

It's stupid but I miss you. It sounds so weird because it's not like you ever went away. I guess it's just harder because you lived with me but you act like a lodger in the house not like a dad. You just come and go as you please with not a care in the world or a responsibility. It is sad to think that your eighteen-year-old daughter acts more maturely than you do. I don't need you anymore, I never did! All I need is my mam. She's the best and you could never add up to her. She raised me, did everything for me and I love her so much which is more than I can say for you!

A letter Anna wrote to sons or daughters of gambling addicts.

Gambling is the worst form of addiction because with alcoholics you can smell it, with drug users you can see the difference in the person and also they feel like crap the next day. But with gambling you can never tell when or if they are doing it.

Dad started to play poker, constantly entering tournaments, playing in casinos. When he was at home it was all he would read about, all he would watch and all he would do on the internet. Another family member and myself confronted him but he flipped. He was completely in denial and when gamblers are like that there is nothing you can do.

The best advice I would give is to go to meetings for spouses of gamblers, go to your school counsellor or to one outside of school. It's confidential at the end of the day but it is good to talk about it because otherwise you get angry and take it out on other people. But don't leave it be the topic of your conversation either because then you get as obsessed with the person, as the person who is gambling. Stick by the other people dealing with the gambler. Don't be disheartened because even if you are in the situation for four or five years you will get out of it and you will move on, and thinking about that will keep you going. I'm in the situation still but I'm in a better frame of mind because I'm now focusing on my life and getting out of the situation soon.

The Follow Up...

My role as Anna's counsellor was to recognise the immediate steps needed to help Anna and also to recognise that the answers lay primarily outside of the school. I referred Anna and her mother to the Local HSE Addiction Services, which offer family members counselling and an advisory service. The help and advice provided by the HSE was extremely useful for both Anna and her mother. It helped to empower them, to give them back control of their own lives. The weekly meetings offered huge support and the sense that they were not on their own.

The focus was moved from her father back onto Anna herself. Her confidence grew as she felt she was doing something to help her mother and their situation. Anna may not have been able to stop her father gambling, but with the essential support she has regained control over her own life.

Coping with addictions can be complicated, for the person who is directly affected and for those who care about them. It can take months, even years, to break a habit that is destroying them. It can also destroy families. I have seen many cases where parents become sick with worry and fear. It changes the dynamic in the home when aggression, dishonesty and disinterest take over. It changes the dynamic in the classroom when lack of motivation, depression and lack of concentration prevent learning from taking place. It can cause heart-breaking and dangerous consequences.

For all concerned it is a continuous battle. It often takes the intervention of an addiction counsellor or a period attending an addiction centre. Both of these are accessed through a referral by the student's GP.

Frequently I meet students who will admit to smoking weed / hash and proudly claim,

It's only weed. I won't get addicted. It doesn't really affect me.

I couldn't disagree more. The change in personality is very evident. Addiction, by its very nature is progressive and harmful.

In schools, we need to continue to educate young people about the devastating price it exacts on individuals, families and communities. We must continue to encourage appropriate decision making and to offer support and advice.

Every member of the school team, from students and parents, to teachers and management, play an important role in the endeavour to address addiction. The school policy on drug and alcohol should reflect this.

Final Thought:

Certain instances demand intervention. It can be met with rejection, anger or fear. The counsellor must remain focused and act with conviction.

FOR STUDENTS

Seek help early.
You are not to blame for what others do.
You are not on your own.
Your parent's / friend's addiction is not your responsibility.
Contact your local Alateen support group.

FOR PARENTS

Don't assume your son / daughter is on drugs because they are moody.
If you suspect drug abuse, don't panic.
Seek advice soon.
Counselling, treatment and advice is offered by your local HSE and GP.
Try to keep communication open, especially with the school.
Encourage involvement in sport and extra-curricular activities.
Praise their achievements.
Encourage positive decision-making.

FOR THE PASTORAL TEAM

The introduction of new legislation in April 2014 – *The Children First Bill:*

1. Requires organisations providing services to children to keep children safe.
2. Requires defined categories of persons (mandated persons – the Designated Liaison Person) to report child protection concerns over a defined threshold to the Child and Family Agency.

Familiarise yourself with this new legislation and procedures.
Familiarise yourself with the school's drug / alcohol policy.
If you recognise signs, express your concerns.
Trust your gut instinct.
Document changes in behaviour or incidents.
Encourage the student to get help from the appropriate professional – the Guidance Counsellor must be the first point of contact.
Insist that someone stays with a student presenting with physical symptoms.
Remember you can only help those who want help.

Further Information...

Useful Websites

www.alcoholicsanonymous.ie

Alcoholics Anonymous (AA) is a self-supporting group of men and women who all have a desire to end their addiction to alcohol. Through meetings they share experiences and hope, in order to help themselves and others.The AA also provides professionals with information about Alcoholics Anonymous.

www.al-anon-ireland.org

Al-Anon offers understanding and support for families and friends of problem drinkers in an anonymous environment.
Alateen is part of Al-Anon and is for young people, aged 12 - 17 inclusive, who are affected by a problem drinker. Teenagers come together to share their experience in order to gain a better understanding of alcoholism and to lessen its impact on their lives.

Email: *info@al-anon-ireland.org*

www.drugs.ie

Drugs.ie offers a directory of drug and alcohol services which offer information, education and support.

HSE Drugs and Alcohol National Helpline: 1800 459 459
Confidential Email Support Service: *helpline@hse.ie*

www.gamblersanonymous.ie

Gambler's Anonymous Ireland (GA) is a self-supporting group of men and women who all have a desire to end their addiction to gambling. Through meetings they share experiences and hope, in order to help themselves and others.

Email: *info@gamblersanonymous.ie*

Chapter 2
Anxiety & Stress

Dandelion in seed
Faced with adverse and ill winds, the dandelion in seed must be resourceful and resilient.

Anxiety & Stress

One of the most common issues to arise in the life of any teenager, boy or girl, is anxiety. It affects us all at some stage in our lives and can be prompted by numerous triggers, such as stress of exams, a traumatic event, worrying about something that has yet to happen or simply being over-tired. Sometimes boys, or girls, can have unrealistic expectations of their goals or achievements and their responses will be determined by the level of their self-esteem. Anxiety can present itself in a number of different ways. It can often be experienced as a lump in the throat or butterflies in the stomach. The most common symptoms that I have seen in school are panic attacks and crying.

It can be very debilitating and the student can often feel isolated, terrified and misunderstood. When anxiety becomes prolonged, the panic attacks that arise can prevent participation in everyday life and activities.

However anxiety can be managed and dealt with. In order to change our reactions to stress and anxiety we need first to understand why it is present and to recognise how we are dealing with it and what changes we can make.

The time it takes to learn how to cope with anxiety will depend on the severity of the anxiety. In most cases the student can work with the Guidance Counsellor to change their behaviours and thinking and reduce the level of stress caused. However, there may be situations when the student would benefit from working specifically with a Cognitive Behavioural Therapist (CBT). Their aim is to help clients understand how negative thoughts and feelings can influence behaviour. All Guidance Counsellors have a list of recommended local counsellors and psychologists who specialise in behavioural therapy. They can also be found on the Irish Association for Counselling and Psychotherapy website: *www.counsellingdirectory.ie.*

Only those individuals who are specifically trained should undertake to work with students suffering from anxiety and stress, as there is often an underlying issue. It is not a condition that can be resolved overnight.

The students' stories that follow range from mild anxiety to very severe anxiety and are often compounded by other issues.

Possible Signs Of Anxiety & Stress To Look Out For:

Frequent crying

Hyperventilating

Appearing flushed - fast heart beat

Panic attacks

Trembling

Headaches and stomach aches

Worry and fear

Disturbed sleep

Introducing Jillian... Aged 15...

Jillian's parents came to me during a parent-teacher meeting, with concerns that she was suffering from anxiety and stress. She would spend hours on her homework, stressing out over the smallest of details. She had always been a worrier but by her second year in school her anxiety had grown so much that it was causing her to have panic attacks. They usually lasted just a few seconds and no one was aware of them happening. But as time went on they became longer, more pronounced and the physical symptoms were too obvious to hide. She frequently left class upset and crying, worrying about what her classmates would think of her. Her friends grew more and more worried, not knowing what to do to help her.

One minute she would laugh; the next she would cry. She was a girl who expressed herself dramatically and openly. She was a perfectionist. Working with her was not easy. She would take one step forward and ten steps back. Some days I believed she was coping well and learning to change how she thought and acted, but I was worried about her state of mind. There seemed to be a much deeper problem than exam anxiety.

The Approach I Used...

To help Jillian to reduce the panic attacks and calm herself down I started by teaching her to control her breathing. It is a technique which I call GBT.

Step 1: Ground Yourself. Sit back into the chair, both feet on the ground and relax your shoulders.
This initial step gave Jillian the security of feeling supported. Her legs stopped trembling and by dropping her shoulders she began to unwind.

Step 2: Breathe Slowly. Concentrate on taking slower and deeper breaths. All students suffering from anxiety present with shallow breathing, which in itself causes more panic and hyperventilation. By making them aware of it, they learn how to control it. In Jillian's case this took time, as she was often quite hysterical. On a number of days I had to get her to breathe into a paper bag to calm her down.

Step 3: Think positively. Change any negative thoughts into positive ones. Aim to find three new positive aspects of your life each day. On paper, this seems straightforward; in practice, it is the one step in the process which I have found is the most difficult to change.
Jillian would say:

There is nothing positive.
I don't have friends.
I don't like myself.

20

I asked her to write down these statements along with five more. I told her we were going to find at least one statement that we could turn into a positive one before the bell went for the next class. I had to be firm and patient until we achieved that goal. One positive is all that is needed to start the process.

Repeating this three-step process allowed Jillian to regain control over her thoughts and to bring her back into the present moment. It is also something she can do in any place at any time when she feels a panic attack coming on.

During each appointment we discussed all the issues causing her anxiety, her emotions, her fears and her self-doubt. Because of the time constraints working against me and my concern for her mental health I met with Jillian's parents and referred her to her GP and from there she was referred to the local Child and Adolescent Mental Health Services (CAMHS).

Jillian's anxiety was to worsen before it got better. It was to take over a year to get to the root of her issues. Her story is detailed and it was a long road for her, her parents and her friends. Before she left the school she wrote her account of what she had experienced. She was now 17.

Jillian's Story... Her own account...

When I first began to write this I thought it would be simple; I was wrong. I said to myself that this was a great way of finally getting closure on everything that happened in the past, but unfortunately I didn't realise how hard it was to even think about when I was thirteen years old and I finally broke. One minute I was standing outside waiting to go to my next class and the next I was doubled over in tears. It was like, all the feelings I kept hidden away finally found a way out. I was taken immediately to a counsellor in my school.

To be perfectly honest I think my mind has blocked out the majority of my first three years in secondary school and I'm glad it has. To say that I was ashamed of who I was would be an understatement. I hated myself. I hated the girl who used to stare at me in every mirror I passed. She wasn't me. She wasn't who I wanted to be. She was a seven year old girl afraid of her own shadow. She was where it all started.

I had been to so many doctors about my anxiety and panic attacks that I had given up every ounce of hope. I just started to accept that I was crazy, even though I was far from that. I was slowly sinking into a depression; a depression where all I wanted to do was cry, sleep and hurl abuse at my reflection. I suppose I should say also that YES I did on some occasions cause harm to myself. It was my way of venting my anger out on something solid, something real. Although at times I couldn't tell the difference. I REGRET everything I did to myself, but at the time it was the only thing I could do.

I lost friends; they left because they "couldn't deal with me". I was distraught. I hated being alone, yet at the same time I didn't want people to see me, especially the person I was then. I hid in corners and in the comfort of my bedroom and all because I was afraid of the people who walked by me, afraid of their stares. My panic attacks were becoming more frequent and more traumatising. I was eventually referred to my doctor who told me that I was most likely suffering from severe anxiety, but should be evaluated by a professional just in case.

I was sick of being told the same thing. "You're going through puberty. You're a teenager, that's natural".
I refused to depend on a pill to make me feel more comfortable with being who I am. I walked out of that appointment with one goal. I was just going to learn how to be myself.

I started to spend time with girls who had the same interests I did. The friends I made accepted me for who I was. They never once passed judgement on what happened in the past. They told me I could always come to them and I believed them, I trusted them. I slowly came more and more out of my shell. I became a part of the school community. I involved myself in extra-curricular activities, tapped into talents I didn't know I possessed.

I learned about parts of my past that I had long forgotten, that were attributed to being the main cause of my anxiety. Knowing that there was a reason all along helped me realise and come to terms with everything that had happened. I knew when it started, I was seven. The seven year old girl I was so afraid of was me, and both of us no longer had any reason to be afraid. We were free.

I'd like to say that I haven't had a bad day in over two years, but I would be lying. I still have days when I feel anxious and afraid; where I feel nauseated and just want to be left alone, but they are just occasional days now.

Everyone has their off days. I'm just like everyone. I don't need to be afraid of what I feel anymore. I can be sad, happy, excited, angry and pretty much any emotion, but the one I love feeling the most is content, because that's exactly what I am now, writing this. I am content with all things me. It does get better. Trust me.

The Follow Up...

Jillian never spoke about what had happened when she was seven. It never came up during our sessions. When I asked her parents they told me there had been a death in the family. It is quite possible that her anxiety was caused by this traumatic event but was only triggered during her teenage years. As a child she did not have the ability to understand it and closed her mind to thinking about it.

The GBT technique was the best approach I could have used with Jillian. It worked because it gave her the opportunity to stop her thoughts racing, to stop her body trembling and it allowed her to become more aware of herself. Once she had grasped it we could then move on to taking each worry and fear individually. After six weeks of systematically writing out the negatives and increasing the positives, I had reached a point where I knew she needed further intervention by a psychiatrist. I also knew I had done all I could to help her. I found this case very difficult. It tested my patience and increased my frustration because progress was slow and tedious.

During her last two years in school she saw many doctors and therapists and tried many treatments. She was often sceptical of the help she received but the combination of treatments started to work. The panic attacks continued but not to the same severity. She was able to function in school and managed to sit her Leaving Certificate and achieved a place on the course she wanted.

I know that she still struggles with anxiety and may always find social situations difficult. My hope is that as she is faced with problems she will draw on the skills she learned in school and can recognise the power of positive thinking and talking.

Introducing Grace... Aged 15...

If I could bottle the goodness, the kindness and the generous spirit that is Grace, I would! Despite coming to me because of her shyness and anxiety issues, she was the girl with the biggest smile, the brightest eyes and the gentlest ways. Grace suffered from social anxiety. She was terrified of being asked a question in class or having to speak out loud. She felt most comfortable away from the limelight with her own group of friends, where she could be herself.

She didn't fear school. She enjoyed it. She was very personable and caring. But when it came to any type of group involvement or when she felt the attention on herself she would clam up. Her heart would race and pound so loudly she thought others could hear it. A pain would travel from her stomach right up to her chest. She would feel herself go red with embarrassment and her lips became so dry that she couldn't speak.

Why was it that a girl so content in her own circle and happy in her life could feel so self-conscious and anxious at times? She wanted to be like everyone else in her class who appeared to have no difficulty speaking or interacting with others. In fact, she was just like so many of her peers but she did not realise it.

The Approach I Used...

During the time I worked with Grace, we concentrated on the positive things in her life and all that she had to offer. Through writing and setting herself tasks like putting up her hand in class when she knew an answer or talking to a different person each day she gradually began to find and hear her voice again. In order to reinforce this positivity she kept a diary each week. She could look back on those positive achievements each weekend, giving her courage to build on these moments in the following week.

The following is a sample of an exercise she completed during a counselling appointment.

What I like about me:

My positive attitude in life.
My understanding of different people.
I help people out when they are in trouble.
I'm kind to others.
My personality with different people.

The things I do well:

Helping people.
Being nice and friendly to others.
Playing with my brothers and sisters.
Listening to others.

What I would change about me:

Talk more-feel more comfortable with myself as a person.
Show people who I really am.
Be able to show my feelings and not bottle them up.
How could I see myself as a more confident person?

If I could be anybody else I would be..

A person who talks a lot.
Doesn't worry what others think.
Feel happy when talking in groups.
Know who I am as a person.
Be more comfortable talking in class.

Knowing the student and establishing a relationship with her, were two key factors in helping her to write these lists. By prompting Grace to enhance key words, I urged her to develop her thoughts and feelings. I asked questions such as:

How are you positive?
How do you help others?
What would make you feel more comfortable?
Describe the feeling you get. What part of you hurts the most?

This written exercise works very well with younger students who are still learning to express themselves. It also portrays the 'child' in the teenager, struggling with change and social interaction.

Two years later, Grace wrote the following letter. Her description of her anxiety is now more refined and thoughtful. It is reflective of a 17-year-old girl becoming a young adult.

Looking Back

Looking back I wonder how I managed to get out of that place. It was a time of deep uncertainty in my life. The feeling of being trapped by what your mind is telling you. "You can't do this. You are not good enough." It was like fighting a constant battle. Anxiety was controlling my life not me. I wondered was I the only one that felt that deep fear in my heart, a fear of even speaking out in a crowd. "Why me?" was always in my mind. I had no control over my own anxiety that is what scared me the most! My positive attitude with life was keeping me strong.

Looking back you get through your life by the strong and encouraging people behind you! It took me two years to control my own anxiety and be myself. I eventually came to terms with believing in myself and not just the gentle voice in the back of the classroom, I wanted to be me! We all serve a different purpose in this life and I knew anxiety was not my purpose.

Anxiety was the hardest thing so far to deal with in my life, but to be who I am today has shown me that people have to believe in themselves, you can do it! Try not to give into that negative voice in your head, be yourself that is all you can be. I feel I won the battle with anxiety. It left me and I am so happy today that I can be myself. Next year I hope to go to college and move on to the next stage of my life and never let anxiety ever control me again.

It was a dark place for me but I found my path. There are certain people you can't ever forget and that person to me was my Guidance Counsellor in school, I am who I am today because of her and I will be forever grateful. Life is so good now and people respect you for the power to be able to be yourself. I know you can because I did it. I always remember these words "you are never alone". Anxiety is a very hard thing but you can stop it.

The Follow Up...

Grace worked hard on her self-esteem and confidence to fight her anxiety. Over the course of five to six weeks she formed positive habits that proved she could get involved in class or group activity.

With encouragement and guidance she completed small tasks of saying hello to someone new, looking someone in the eye and raising her hand for one word answers. With each task came confidence, a confidence that developed as the tasks were increased. Once she completed the most feared task of speaking in class and in groups the anxiety subsided.

Many shy students feel invisible in social situations.They are not talkers. They do not get the same attention that confident, out-going or boisterous students get. So they retreat inwards and protect themselves to remain invisible for fear of making mistakes. They often underachieve in school and do not reach their potential as a result. I recognised this in Grace and wanted to help her find her voice and know that she was heard. I wanted her to see what I saw in her. On reflection, the counselling was very effective for Grace because I could empathise fully with her. As an adult, I still find it daunting to speak in public and make my own voice heard. So in this instance it was a pleasant challenge.

When a student comes for counselling without being sent, they are ready. They want change and they embrace it. I knew that the most effective approach would have to be gentle, full of praise and reassurance.

Grace went on to college where she still got nervous when she had to make presentations or get involved in discussions. It is not something she likes doing but knows that she has to. Ironically, she now finds herself back again in a classroom. She is no longer the student fearful of raising her hand, but is the teacher talking!

Introducing Patrick... Aged 17...

Patrick was a shadow of his former self when I met him first. He was gaunt, pale and very withdrawn. He was not sleeping and had lost his appetite. He had given up all the sports he used to do and was finding it hard to continue with his music classes. He was very down in himself and spoke about "not wanting to be here anymore". It was not a statement of intention to do harm to himself but rather an expression of just how low he was feeling. He had stopped going out with his friends, preferring to be on his own at home.

Patrick's anxiety was triggered by an illness he had during the summer before fifth year. He was diagnosed with stomach problems and eventually clinical depression. Each condition exacerbated the other. I met Patrick once a week, working on coping skills and self-esteem building. Through his doctor, he was referred on to a Cognitive Behavioural Therapist who also worked in the area of alternative medicine.

Patrick's account of his anxiety is very honest, clear and practical. Through his own words he best describes the struggle he faced for a long time.

The Approach I Used...

During the appointments we looked at the issues of self-esteem and coping skills separately and we came up with possible solutions to each one. We made two lists;

List 1: The physical effects of anxiety / depression:
e.g., Lack of sleep, no appetite, weight loss, tired, aches and pains.

List 2: The psychological effects:
e.g., feeling down, no motivation, wanting to be alone, negative thinking.

Having discussed each one, Patrick's task was to make small changes to his day, to find a routine and to stick to it.
For example:
Issue 1 = Lack of sleep

Trial solution =

- Go for a short walk early in the evening.
- Turn off the computer an hour before bed.
- Do not drink tea or coffee in the evening.
- Read for twenty minutes before lights out.
- Write down anything that is worrying you and tackle it tomorrow.
- Go to bed at the same time each night.

When we are anxious and feeling down everything seems confused and disordered. By bringing back routine and small tasks we regain an order to our actions and our thoughts. This process gave Patrick a sense of accomplishment and purpose.

He wrote the following piece which aptly portrays his own understanding of the benefits of talking to someone and trying out what best worked for him.

Patrick's Story...

Stress and anxiety are very important. They help keep us out of danger. But prolonged stress can cause problems with sleeping, eating, socialising and coping. I would have to say that having anxiety is a very unpleasant feeling. It is a feeling of apprehension or fear and sometimes you might not even know what is causing it which can make the feeling worse. It is a feeling you get almost every day. You have to fully overcome your anxiety before it will go away but short term you can find little things to help you cope with it.

I tried having a warm relaxing bath one night, it wasn't for me. Stay patient; try something else the next day. I went for a walk. It was ok. The next day I took out my trumpet and I found it to be very therapeutic and relieved a lot of tension that I was carrying around with me. Hitting a sliotar was another thing I found great.

All these relaxation techniques are great. They keep your head above water. However they will not solve your anxiety issues. Take the step in talking to a counsellor. In my own experience it took me quite a while to deal with my anxiety and stress. I was always excellent in school and had plenty of friends but my anxiety struck me when I missed a few weeks of school due to illness. I was absolutely terrified of going back to school. I tried every day to go back but it was very difficult and I sometimes broke down in tears. Eventually, after many attempts I succeeded with the help of my parents and the Guidance Counsellor.

Unfortunately I was behind in so much. It was overwhelming. My friends didn't know how to react as I was visibly thinner and paler and they distanced themselves from me, no fault of theirs because it wasn't intentional but it's the only way they knew how to react. Of course this made things worse for me and I felt like I lost everything and it seemed impossible to get it all back.

I was struggling to catch up with material I had missed even though teachers were giving me extra help. I was also falling behind in what the class was doing at that time for the first time in my life. It felt like I was stuck in a circle and there was no way out.

Any time before going out or going to a party the anxiety levels were sky-high. I wasn't at all comfortable with myself. I really didn't want to go. After a huge struggle with myself I always went. I won't say I enjoyed them but I knew the longer I left it the worse it would get.

When I had missed a lot of school and was trying to catch up I used to say, 'I have so much to catch up on. There is too much.' After a while I learned how to break it down. I was overwhelming myself by saying it was 'school' that was the problem. I broke it down to one subject at a time. This is far less overwhelming. By identifying exactly what is causing your anxiety you can tackle it much easier and it doesn't seem so big.

Once you have learned how to deal with your anxiety you will be a greater person for doing so. It will make you stronger and you will be more capable of dealing with situations in the future. You get to learn lots of things about yourself that you might otherwise never have known and most importantly you will feel good about yourself.

The Follow Up...

Patrick finally found treatment for his stomach problems and over time his health improved. With the change in his daily routine and concentrating on completing small tasks his anxiety levels began to decrease. The building blocks for Patrick's success were to set achievable goals and to empower him to move forward by completing daily tasks. His confidence grew as each symptom lessened and he began to return to a more self-assured young man.

He used the support of counselling in school and the support given by his parents, teachers and friends, which encouraged him to keep going. He has overcome some of his doubts and insecurities and the road ahead is now less daunting.

Reflection...

Stress is a common factor in all our lives. It can occur when we have to make decisions, meet people, complete tasks, meet deadlines or do something new. Children and young adults are still developing cognitively and as a result are not sufficiently developed to be able to process traumas and stress. As a result they tend to blame themselves for the consequences of it.

A little stress is a good thing, a lot is not. When stress is prolonged we become anxious. We worry about "what ifs" and things that might never happen. We experience physical changes like sweating or nervous stomachs. We lack sleep and feel tired all the time. It can be exhausting. As well as the physical symptoms of anxiety there are many different feelings associated with it:

Loss of control;
Feeling overwhelmed;
Thinking negatively;
Feeling confused and forgetful;
Feeling lethargic.

There are three key steps to regaining control over anxiety.

1. Write it down:

Write a list of what needs to be done, prioritise it and start TODAY. Start small and set realistic goals. Treating yourself when you complete a goal is very important. When a goal is achieved it builds confidence and encourages us to keep going. Cross it off the list and move on to the next. The physical act of writing helps to organise thoughts which can appear less daunting in black and white.

2. Talk it out:

When we put words on our anxieties and stress they are often confused and exaggerated. Talking through each issue brings clarity from another's perspective.

3. Change how you react to situations:

If we think negatively, we react negatively. If we think positively, we react positively. Rebuild self-esteem through a series of manageable and comfortable goals each week.

The counselling process is collaborative. The counsellor must guide the student. Through a series of tasks the student is empowered to become independent again.

FOR STUDENTS

When you think 'I can't' say to yourself 'I can'.
Make a 'To-Do' list each day.
Keep a journal-write down a 'worry of the day' and get it out of your head.
Reflect each day on what worked well or what didn't work well. What could you change?
Get involved in a sport or hobby to take your mind off the anxiety.
Go for a walk.
Learn how to control your breathing.
Relaxation therapies like massage can be very beneficial.

FOR PARENTS

Panic attacks that continue to recur need further investigation.
Encourage healthy eating and exercise to reduce stress.
With regards to exam anxiety, reassure that they can only do their best.
Encourage realistic expectations.
Provide a calm and positive atmosphere at home.
Encourage involvement in voluntary work. Helping others can really boost self-esteem.
Try to help your son / daughter to focus on today and on taking small steps.

FOR THE PASTORAL TEAM

Professional help should be sought where appropriate.
Teach the student how to manage their time. Break down large tasks into smaller manageable ones.
Encourage the student to use positive statements eg; 'I can do this'.
Encourage the student to focus on the task rather than the time.
Set goals that are attainablae.
Encourage writing about how they are feeling.
Help the student to learn how to relax, through 'time out' activities like walking or swimming, listening to music or taking a bath.

Further Information...

Useful Websites

www.spunout.ie

Spunout was created by a group of young adults. It promotes positive well-being by offering relevant and non-judgemental advice to assist other young people in making informed decisions.

Email: *info@spunout.ie*

www.teenline.ie

Teenline Ireland is a Freephone service for young adults. Their aim is to provide a listening service for young people who may be suffering from anxiety, stress or worry.

Teenline Helpline: 1800 833 634

www.headstrong.ie

Headstrong is the national centre for youth mental health. Its aim is to empower young people to develop the skills and resilience to cope with mental health challenges. It also provides resources for teachers and parents.

Email: *info@headstrong.ie*

Chapter 3
Bereavement & Loss

Lily
Simple and pure, the lily is associated with remembrance and sympathy.

Bereavement & Loss

We cannot shield ourselves from bereavement - it is an inevitable reality of life which we all eventually experience. It can be particularly difficult for adolescents, as they are already trying to come to terms with forming relationships and understanding themselves. They are caught between childhood and adulthood and between being dependent and independent. Therefore coping with loss can be extremely challenging. Added to their normal insecurities, they now experience the loss of security and familiarity. When a family member or friend dies it can feel that their whole world has died with them.

Like adults, they need to experience the process of grief and all the stages that it involves. Sometimes, these stages don't always follow a pattern and for many there can be a combination of stages. The most common reactions to the loss of a loved one will be shock, denial, anger, guilt and acceptance.

Within this chapter I have chosen also to include the loss of a parent by separation or divorce as it is also considered a bereavement. The process of separation is, in itself, a grieving process. It is like a death in the family. Normality breaks down and is replaced with insecurity. In younger students particularly, I have seen a preference for parents to stay together despite the unhappiness that is present. Younger teenagers have a greater need to hold on to what they know and the fear of change and the unknown can be too much for them. Older teenagers on the other hand, know and understand the reality of the situation better. While they may still hope for parental reconciliation, they recognise the need for separation and at times it can bring relief, bringing stability back into the home.

Possible Signs of Loss to Watch Out For:

Aggression
Loneliness
Confusion
Helplessness
Sleeplessness
Loss of appetite
Over-eating
Loss of energy
Loss of concentration
Loss of interest in everyday tasks

Introducing Lisa... Aged 13...

Lisa said goodbye to her father and left for school, not knowing it would be the last time she would see him. Her father was a single parent and they had shared a very special bond. Her father died suddenly that day. The shock was overwhelming for Lisa, who at such a young age and an only child found it impossible to understand. Not only had she lost her father but she lost her home also. Her whole life as she knew it had changed.

Lisa was taken in and cared for by her relatives. She struggled to come to terms with the enormity of her grief and sadness. She became angry at her father for leaving her and causing her such pain.

The Approach I Used...

In our weekly meetings she spoke endlessly of her time with her father and how much she missed him. She cried throughout and asked why it had happened and why he had left her. She was still very much in a state of shock.

I decided to use an activity called *The Memory Jar.*

(Items needed: a clear jar which the student chooses, coloured chalk, salt and a sheet of sandpaper.)

It can be a very useful way of helping younger teenagers to express their emotions after losing a parent or grandparent. It is a jar filled with layers of salt, each layer coloured with different colour chalks (Rubbing the chalk with sandpaper over separate piles of salt colours it.) As it is poured into the jar by the student it must be kept very still and not shaken. The result is a rainbow of bright colours, each colour represents a feeling or memory they associate with the person who has passed away.

This approach allowed me to ask questions about why she chose a colour or what memory it brought up. Without realising it Lisa was creating a way of grieving by talking through the shock, loss and hurt.

The following is a sample piece she wrote after completing *The Memory Jar.* One of the colours she chose was yellow, as it reminded her of her father's 'heart of gold'.

"How I Feel" by Lisa

Since my dad died I feel my heart is broken in half. It's like a pain that never goes away and I don't think it ever will. I know crying won't bring him back but sometimes I can't keep it in so I go to my room and I listen to the songs my dad liked and cry my eyes out.

People say it gets easier. It does but not too much. Not a day goes by without me thinking of my dad. I feel really hurt. My dad and I shared everything together. He had a heart of gold. My dad is gone. I want him now more than ever. It's really hard but I try to hide it. Some people can see straight through me. They know when I am upset. Now he is dead I think it's only hitting me. I hope to see my dad in heaven someday.

I encouraged Lisa to write regularly to her father telling him of all that had changed and how her life was now. It was another way for her to communicate with him and to keep his memory alive.

Lisa wrote a note to her father.

I thought you would live forever.
I miss you. I miss our life as it was. You were always so good to me. You always listened and minded me.
I don't know why this happened. I don't know where you are - only that you are not here. I hope you are with your parents some place that's nice. I think about you every day and night. I am so lonely at night. I will never forget you and I will always love you.

The Follow Up...

The Memory Jar proved to be effective in a number of ways. Firstly, the physical act of creating a memorial to her father was therapeutic. In doing so she had a very personal tribute to her relationship with him that she could keep and cherish. Secondly, the colours held meaning and the jar itself became a unique and intimate link with her father.

Due to the change in her living arrangements, Lisa was moved to another school closer to her new home. It was an unfortunate but necessary move. I was concerned that there had been too many changes for her to cope with. But it was outside of my control. I made contact with her new school to express my concerns and to request any continued support they could offer her. I made a follow up phone call to liaise with her new Guidance Counsellor and to determine how she was settling in. Lisa was happy to continue with the counselling and was benefitting from the time she was offered. She was adjusting slowly to her new school, making new friends and living with her relatives. She was still in the early stages of grieving for her father and it would be an on-going and life-long process.

Lisa was forced to grow up far too quickly having lost everything she knew and loved. Her life as she had known it changed forever. Some children have a resilience that we as adults struggle to find in traumatic times. I hope Lisa has this resilience.

Introducing Clodagh... Aged 15...

Clodagh's father died when she was fifteen, after a long battle with cancer. She was extremely close to her dad and loved him deeply. He was the one she connected with and felt closest to in the family. She could talk to him and tell him her fears and worries. He was a gentle, kind and loving man. He always looked out for her and was there when she needed him. She had a tough childhood, tougher than most. When he died, her world fell apart. She missed him dreadfully and felt so alone. Everything changed at home. Her mother withdrew into herself and struggled to cope. Clodagh had so many worries and so many questions. *Who would now take care of her? Who would she turn to? Who would make decisions in the home? How would she cope without him?*

All of her brothers and sisters reacted differently to his death. Some became withdrawn, some acted out aggressively and some, like Clodagh, began to talk it out.

The Approach I Used...

I met Clodagh regularly over the following two years. During that time, she cried incessantly. She was sad and lonely. She felt guilty that she couldn't do anything to save him and at the same time she was angry with him for leaving her. She wrote pages and pages of letters and poems, some to her Dad, some to me. At night when she couldn't sleep, she wrote. When she had a free class in school, she wrote. When she should have been doing her homework, she wrote. It helped her work it all out in her own head and gave her a sense of releasing the shock and anxiety.

I persuaded Clodagh to start a *Memory Box*. I wanted to create another opportunity for her to remember her father.

It was to become the place where she would store all her letters and poems and any items that reminded her of her father. In it she included old photographs and mementos.It gave her the chance to talk about her father as she explained why for example she chose a photograph of herself as a young child sitting on his knee. It brought up happy memories of moments with him but also highlighted the reality that he was no longer with her.

In the initial stages of the counselling process I give considerable time to developing the student – counsellor relationship and setting the tone for the subsequent appointments. Using the *Memory Box* not only benefits the student but also me, as the counsellor. It allows me to introduce constructive change and progress into each 40 minute session.

The following poem submitted to the *Memory Box* expresses the pain and sorrow she was experiencing. It reflects the feeling of loneliness and her silent grieving.

A Whispering Tear

I whisper to you hoping you would comfort me
Each tear I shed for you, no pain has melted my sorrow.
I call out to you, but no answer do I hear
But instead a lonely cry from far below.

I sit here in a crowded room
Friends smile and pass
But I sit here in a dark circle
But no one I can hold will last.

Many lines have I written
But to whom and why
Like a gift which is unopened
Piece by piece the truth will lie.

Never known to many
The pain I carried with my name
The tears I cried in unforgettable places
Where there was no one - I look around,
There's nothing the same.

The Follow Up...

When her Leaving Certificate ended I referred Clodagh on for counselling outside of school. She only went for three sessions as she found it too difficult to trust anyone else. This is a common problem brought on by the nature of a school year finishing or holidays beginning. Her father's best friend took on the role of guiding and encouraging her. Her family fell apart after her father's death and all her siblings went their separate ways.

Clodagh herself left Ireland to train to be a nurse. It was a decision that was brave and considered. She qualified as a nurse and now cares for the sick. Her choice of profession was partly shaped by the loss she experienced at 15. It has proven to be a career to which she can bring her own life experience and empathy. Nursing provides her with personal satisfaction and, to some degree, therapy. The care she offers is, for her, a tangible link with her father.

Introducing Chloe... Aged 15...

Chloe was fifteen when her parents separated. Her father had left the home and everything that was normal had changed. She had two younger siblings. When I met Chloe she was broken-hearted. She was very close to her mother and could see the devastating effect it was having on her. She automatically took on a role of responsibility and stepped into her father's shoes of looking after everyone. She knew it was for the best, but that didn't take away the feelings of deep sadness and loneliness that she was experiencing. She was very angry with her father for letting the family down, for giving up on them and for sacrificing their happiness for his need to be on his own. She kept up a wall of defence and rarely showed her emotions to others in school, which only came out during our weekly appointments.

The Approach I Used...

In the counselling sessions we explored her relationship with both her parents and how their separation had affected her and the whole family. As with all teenagers who experience separation there was a feeling of "being stuck in the middle", negotiating between both parties. Chloe in a sense was grieving for the loss of her father and the adjustments that were forced upon her. It was important that she could talk to him and maintain a relationship with him.

Through talking and writing Chloe found a way of coping and expressing herself. This creative writing soothes her personal pain allowing her to put words on her feelings of anger, confusion and shock. This process works for teenagers especially as it forces them to stop, to think and to understand emotions usually compounded by their stage of development.

My role included:

1.   Listening actively;

2.   Encouraging free expression;

3.   Guiding her in identifying and understanding fears and worries;

4.   Suggesting ways to help her focus and relax when it began to have an effect on her schoolwork and motivation;

5.   Encouraging peer support which plays a huge part in a teenager's development. During a time of uncertainty it can be a very stabilising factor.

Chloe wrote the following poem after her parents separated:

The Questions, No Answers, Not Fair...

Here are some of the questions
You always wanted me to ask,
When my anger was too strong,
And my rage just hadn't passed.
You left your kids confused
And not knowing what was wrong
You left your wife in desperation
And me?
I wrote a song.
A song to ask the questions
That never reached my mouth
A song to fill the emptiness
That leaves me having doubts

Though my anger is still strong
And my rage still hasn't passed.
Your kids are no longer confused
They now know what's going on,
Your wife is no longer desperate
And me? I'm moving on.
I've moved on to ask the questions
That now have reached my mouth
They have filled up most of the emptiness
Though I still have my doubts.

Did you ever think
About what you might lose?
Was it always a case of "it" or "us",
A choice only you could choose?
Did it ever even dawn on you
That we might walk away
Or did you just hold your breath
And hope for one more day?
One more to say you love me
Your words I always loved to hear
You just don't seem to get it
That you're not walking along on air
The Questions, No Answers, Not Fair.

The Follow Up...

Chloe's experience of parental separation forced a new reality upon her. Over the course of her visits to me she accepted that she could not 'fix' the difficulties between her parents. She acknowledged that they were happier living separately but could not accept that her parents' love for her was not diminished. Her mother began to regain some control of the situation and the roles of support and responsibility reverted to her. She continued to struggle with feeling very much alone and down. Her studies and schoolwork were impacted on but she did manage to complete her exams and won her place in university where she is today.

Chloe has continued to attend counselling, now in the Counselling Department in her university. She finds that there are still days when she needs to have a listening ear. She has developed her writing skills and has progressed to journalistic pieces, working occasionally in the world of media.

Reflection...

The grieving process can last a long time, much longer than we often realise. Everyone responds differently to death and it is essential to remember that there is no right or wrong way to grieve. Our responses will be determined by a number of things - the relationship we had with the person who has died, the experiences we have had previously of death and also by the support structures we have around us.

At the best of times, adolescents find it difficult to express their emotions and will often turn to their peers for support, but their peers may not have the resources to help them. So it is vital that they are encouraged to talk it through with an adult whom they trust. In the school setting this can either be the Guidance Counsellor or the Chaplain. Subject teachers and tutors play an important role in monitoring all students in their care and can offer essential insights into classroom performance and behaviour.

There are also a number of specific support programmes offered around the country. The purpose of these is to provide a listening service to assist young people to work through the process of grief and loss, in a safe environment. They are run by individual schools or family support centres. They offer both an individual and a shared experience with others of a similar age.

The programme I have referred students on to is called *Seedlings*. This is a seven-week grief support programme run by Barnardos for children and young people who have suffered loss through bereavement or separation. It has been temporarily postponed while they await funding.

Rainbowsireland run a 12-14-week programme, operated by volunteers from frontline services who have been trained in identifying and meeting the needs of those experiencing grief.

Both programmes are voluntary and have limited places and waiting lists.

Final Thought:

At the heart of counselling is listening. Real listening, with the ears, the eyes and all the senses employed. With bereavement, especially, the client needs the opportunity to be heard. They need to tell of their loss repeatedly and to vocalise it. In doing so they feel their loved one is remembered.

FOR STUDENTS

Take time to cry.
Take one day at a time.
Remember, those you loved want you to be happy.
Get some rest.
Know that the pain does ease.
It is normal to feel angry or guilty, express it.
Keep a Memory Box.
Write a letter to say your goodbye.

FOR PARENTS

Encourage, but don't pressurize your son / daughter to take part in the funeral arrangements.
Allow your son / daughter to ask questions and provide simple and honest answers.
If you silence your grief, your son / daughter will learn to silence theirs.
Remember they may not want to upset you more by talking about their own sadness.
Try not to burden your son / daughter with the difficulties that may be ahead of you.
Take care of yourself. It is easy to neglect oneself during times of loss.
Use the resources around you for support.

FOR THE PASTORAL TEAM

Be patient, the grieving process may take up to two years.
Allow the student to tell the story of the person who has died.
Encourage them to keep a *Memory Box* with thoughts, words and pictures that remind them of those they have lost.
If you become worried that a particular behaviour is persisting, seek professional help for the student.
Remember that we cannot protect them from the reality of death but we can help them to understand and to grieve.
Organise a service of remembrance for students who have lost a loved one through death.

Further Information...

Useful Websites

www.barnardos.ie

Barnardos Bereavement Service is a practical and professional service. It is available in several towns, for children and teenagers who have lost a parent or a sibling through death.

Email: *bereavement@barnardos.ie*

www.rainbowsireland.com

Rainbows Ireland offers a free service to help those affected by loss, as a result of bereavement, separation or divorce. It provides a safe environment in which children and teenagers can talk through their emotions with others of a similar age. This service is available in family centres and schools throughout the country and is given by trained volunteers.

www.teenbetween.ie

Teen Between is a counselling service funded by the Family Support Agency (FSA) which aims to help teenagers cope with their parents' separation or divorce. At present, it operates eight different support centres around the country.

Email: *teenbetween@relationshipsireland.com*
Free Phone Helpline: 1800 303 191

Suggested Reading

Bereavement Information Pack
October 2008

Available to download on:
www.barnardos.ie/.../information-pack/bereavement_october_2008.pdf

Chapter 4
Bullying

Honeysuckle
Obstacles force the honeysuckle to find alternative paths to reach the light and to survive in challenging conditions.

Bullying

Unlike other areas of counselling where students will come themselves, students who are being bullied rarely refer themselves. They are usually referred by their year head, parents, teachers or friends. They are always slow to talk, have difficulty trusting that anyone can help and always express embarrassment at being upset. Their greatest fear is that they will be called a 'rat' for telling their story.

In all the bullying cases I have worked there are tell-tale signs that a student is being bullied. They differ from person to person but they are present.

Bullying is a real and very complex problem and is rarely resolved quickly. It can take many forms and by its nature is a repeated act that can have devastating effects. It can include:

Name calling;
Abusive texting and phone calls;
Cyber bullying on 'Facebook', 'MSN' or 'Twitter';
Physical aggression and fighting;
'Dirty looks';
Exclusion.

Possible Signs of Bullying to Look Out For:

Not wanting to come to school

Absenteeism

Panic attacks

Stomach pains /headaches

Being withdrawn and quiet

Underperforming in schoolwork

Presenting with bruises or scrapes

Introducing Cathy... Aged 13...

Cathy was a first-year student. She was gentle, shy and quiet. She stood out as being different from the norm with her pale skin, big blue eyes and long red hair. She had a close group of friends and like all those around her, wanted to fit in. Her transition from primary school was not easy. She had come from a small single-sex country school to a large and mixed secondary school. The adjustment was enormous – new classmates, new teachers, new subjects, new uniform, new building, new rules and a new routine. She found it very daunting. Having her friends around her to chat with, and compare experiences, helped a lot.

But by the October midterm everything began to change. One by one her friends seemed to disappear. She felt more alone each day. She became the centre of jokes passed in class. The looks, the snide remarks, and the sniggering all became too much for her. Her parents, who had seen the unhappiness and the tears, contacted the school. They were considering moving her to another school. I met Cathy a couple of times, working on re-building her self-esteem and confidence. She wanted to be happy and to feel she belonged. She wanted to believe in herself again.

The Approach I Used...

With any case of bullying it is important to act quickly. Once a victim of bullying opens up, they need help and it needs to be supportive. It is about teaching them the skills to recognize their own personal strengths and power to survive, rather than intervening in such a way as to make the situation worse. It is about empowering them to be assertive rather than passive.

Each week Cathy and I concentrated on four key elements:

1.   Looking at where she was at now;

2.   Looking at where she wanted to be;

3.   Discussing ways to deal with the bullies;

4.   Affirming her personal values and beliefs.

Week 1: I asked Cathy to complete a *Me Badge* - as a way of expressing how she felt. She used words like 'shy', 'quiet', 'sad', 'lonely' and 'afraid' to describe herself. We discussed each feeling and its effect on her physically e.g. nervous stomach, headaches and tearfulness. Building Cathy's resilience and inner – strengths would be the target for our sessions as we moved forward.

Week 2: Cathy devised a new me badge, to express how she wanted to feel. She included 'happy', 'confident', 'pretty', 'with friends'. I gave her small tasks to complete to help her focus on the positive aspects of herself. For example;
Looking in the mirror each morning and giving herself a compliment;
Making eye contact or smiling at someone each day;
Taking part in a new activity - she chose the Girl Guides.

Again, the key to Cathy's progress was allowing her to uncover her own strengths which would encourage her to be more assertive.

Week 3: As she felt stronger we discussed her options when faced with bullying and how she would react to those who bullied her. Cathy understood that avoiding the bully was an assertive act. It was a decision of her own and empowering. This choice shifted the balance of power back to Cathy.

Week 4: As her confidence grew she began to realise that in fact she liked who she was and was most comfortable surrounded by like-minded people. She began to find what all teenagers strive for, a sense of belonging.

Cathy's Story...

Her own account of the bullying she endured:

They are only nice when they want something. They could be lovely one second but when you walk away you can hear them talking about you. I get mocked because of my hair colour. If I'm ever asked anything they stare, laugh and talk about me. I hate it so much. It's the thing they do. It's constant, annoying and embarrasses me a lot. They only do it because they know it affects me and I don't like it. They took my best friend and know I have nothing and now rub it in. "Why isn't she with you, what did you do?"

They only ask because they know she hangs around with them. Last year they were mean to everyone and she couldn't take it so she decided to join them as it was easier. I understand why she did it, it is easier but it just hurts how she mocks, laughs and joins in as they say bad things about me and still tells me she's my friend. She only talks to me when the gang isn't there. I'm sick of them and wouldn't mind moving class but know if I do I won't be friends with her. I'm upset she doesn't talk to me, only about me, but I still want to be her friend.

This is a poem Cathy wrote after counselling had finished and she had worked on rebuilding her self-esteem:

I am just like you
I am in the same school too
I was the one they pointed at and said 'she'
But now I am finally free.

School was not my favourite place
They always seemed to be on my case
They hurt my feelings and much more
Going to school was worse than a chore.

I hated school for a while
But now I am able to smile.
School is no longer a scary place for me
It is where I can be normal and carefree.

I am happy now in school
It actually feels cool.

The Follow Up...

Cathy was pro-active in fighting for her right to be included. Through the counselling process she learned how to respond assertively and to be proud of the person she was and how she looked. She learned the true meaning of friendship and to believe in the values she had grown up with.

Many students in Cathy's situation perceive 'avoidance' of the bully as a form of cowardice. However, in actuality, it is a tremendous signal to the bully of inner-strength and character. Understanding this allowed Cathy to become more resilient. In walking away Cathy left the "victim within herself" behind. She presented a new face to her bullies. It was one they recognised as strong, self-reliant and independent. They no longer had a powerless and passive target. The name-calling gradually came to an end. She made new friends and is finding her place in the school community.

It was important that Cathy was not moved to another school where she would have to cope with new surroundings and new friendships. The solution lay more within herself, than outside.

Introducing John... Aged 15...

The turmoil John had been through first came to my attention when he was in third year. His English teacher passed on an essay he had written which concerned her. The anger and frustration he felt towards those who bullied him was very evident in both his writing and behaviour. He had been prone to the occasional outburst in class which often got him into trouble with his teachers. I liked John. He was always honest and spoke his mind. I found him to be very open to receive help and advice. He never showed fear or sadness. It was through anger that he expressed his emotions.

The Approach I Used...

When I asked John why he thought certain boys were taunting and hurting him he said that they wanted to make him mad and get him into trouble. They enjoyed making fun of him to make the other students laugh. A bully's motivation is to cause **H**urt, **A**nger, **T**rouble or to **E**ntertain. (HATE)

Once he understood that they were controlling him with this behaviour, I asked him if his responses were giving them what they wanted. He realised he was empowering their actions. Before we could venture to change his responses I needed to help John deal with the anger he was feeling towards himself and the bullies. I used a worksheet for this exercise as I have found it helps the student to articulate their feelings. It involves finishing sentences such as:

I lose my temper when ...
I feel angry when ...
I am going to hit the next person who ...
People who tell me what to do ...

Using this activity John became more aware that having suppressed his anger he had caused more stress on his body, a stress that in turn caused stomach aches and tension headaches. As the anger began to subside we then turned our focus to how he would respond the next time he was threatened or intimidated. We used the ARCH method.

Avoid them
Retaliate with aggression
Change the subject by distracting them
Humour

Both the HATE model and ARCH method are part of Brian Lennon's Cool Anger Management Programme (CAM).

John chose to avoid confrontation. He also chose to use his sense of humour as his best method of empowerment.

John's Story...

This is an excerpt from his essay:

The suppressed anger and the feeling in the pit of my stomach as I set off for school, was there once again. I had got the strange feeling a lot lately and as I headed for my bus it was planted in my body again this morning.

I started first year full of excitement just like most people starting a new school. Despite the fact that my best friends had gone to different schools I knew people and wasn't unhappy going to school. First year was a bad year. But it wasn't as bad as what was to come. I had made one friend, Paul. He wasn't as bad as the rest of them and we had similar interests. I was continually taunted with "John's gay" and John's bent", but I had gotten used to it.

Second year was terrible. Once again I got off to a bad start. Paul was moved to a different class. I still had friends outside the class but it seemed the people in the class were using their influence outside the class on my friends.
"He's gay. Don't hang around with him. He's a faggot!!"
These words were started by one particular guy and followed by others. That one person I have nothing but hatred for. As time went on a deep hatred developed inside of me.

The one thing I have learned is that if you don't have what bullies would call "Protectors" (older people to "protect" you), you may be a target. Even yesterday after a football match, I was "started on" by a boy in second year, but I couldn't do anything because he had ten people behind him, I had none!

I'm now in third year in the middle of my exams. Despite the fact that I have come out of school with many bruises inside and outside, despite the fact that I had to pretend to fall in the door one day after school for an excuse for the bruises on my face, I have had a few good moments. Third year hasn't been that bad, but I still have that deep hatred inside for the bullies and as I walk each morning to the bus I will still have that weird and strange feeling in my body.

The Follow Up...

There is a certain bullying phase that begins, for boys, in particular in Second Year. The majority of the issues are resolved by Transition Year. For girls, on the other hand it begins a little later at the end of Second Year. It usually is resolved by the end of Transition Year.

Second Year seems to be the opening chapter of bullying at second level. The reasons may relate to the onset of puberty, physical changes and the structures of power within their social circles. Essentially, it is about ego, self-esteem and power.

When John returned after third year he had grown considerably, both physically and emotionally. He was stronger and taller. The summer had matured him and he no longer felt threatened by others around him. He was more self-assured. He had learned to walk away from fights rather than get involved. He channelled his own aggression into sport and fitness. He didn't need 'Protectors'. He had learned to protect himself and avoid confrontations. In transition year he found a group of friends who were like-minded and in whom he could confide. He no longer had that strange feeling in the pit of his stomach when he passed those who had intimidated him.

While counselling John, I looked beyond the angry young man in front of me, to see the young man I knew he could become. John learned, through counselling, that alternative responses to the bullies would empower him, rather than them.

Introducing Ben... Aged 13...

In primary school he had struggled with friendships and the feeling of being excluded. He found it difficult to maintain friends and always felt on the edge of groups and teams. He hoped this would change when he entered secondary school. But it didn't. Among his new peers he felt even more invisible. To all his teachers he was extremely pleasant, hardworking and a diligent student. He participated in class, spoke when he was asked and offered up suggestions and answers to questions. *So why did he feel so isolated? Why did others mock him when he spoke? Why were they so mean to him when he was so good to others? Why does anyone bully?* It is sometimes hard to find the answers to any of these questions.

Ben had friends – good friends he thought. They liked the same things, spent time together and shared their experiences. This was changing too. He took up music and joined clubs. Outside of school he felt safe and secure. He was himself. He was visible. *Why was school so different for him?* Ben had hoped for a fresh start with his transition to secondary school. He did everything right, joining new clubs and getting involved in hobbies outside of school. But he still remained exposed to new threats of bullying. He became the target of smart comments, mocking and exclusion.

His Year Head referred him for counselling when teachers had observed him as withdrawn and isolated. He would not disclose the names of those who were threatening him. As an only child he did not have a sibling with whom to compare himself to or chat with.

The Approach I Used...

I explained my role to Ben, to offer him support, a safe environment and confidentiality. To ease into the process I focused on building his self-confidence rather than delving into his past experiences and feelings.

It can be difficult for students, young boys especially, to open up in the counselling setting. Therefore it is paramount that the Guidance Counsellor has the skill to:

1. Know how to approach each individual student;

2. Know which approach will best suit the particular student.

Context is a key factor in counselling. Knowing family background, academic achievement, pastimes and student aspirations are all components that shape the approach that will be used.

Ben had learned to hide his feelings to protect himself and found it hard to trust anyone to help him. I affirmed and praised his involvement in activities outside school.

I used worksheets to encourage Ben to explore the positive aspects of his life and each session gave him the task of saying hello to someone, smiling at someone or looking someone in the eye. My goal was to help him develop a sense of no longer being invisible and the awareness that small changes could give him back control.

Ben's Story...

A poem he wrote about being bullied.

Being Bullied

No one wants to be bullied,
It makes you feel unsafe
There is a sudden feeling of fear
As you see the bully coming near.

If you are one of the bystanders
Then think of what it could do
Just step in and you will see
The change that it could do.

So if you are one of the bystanders
Who watch all the strife
Stand by that person the next time
It could change their life.

The Follow Up...

I would have liked more time with Ben. Summer came and he did not return for counselling again. I knew that he was very conscious of leaving a class to attend the Guidance Counsellor. He was concerned that it might draw more attention to him if he continued to attend. This is a situation that occurs predominantly amongst boys in this age group, 13-14-year-olds. They have not developed emotionally to cope with the notion of counselling. They are just not ready and should not be forced to attend. It can also be seen as 'uncool' and can exacerbate forms of exclusion.

The Guidance Counsellor can be proactive, in this regard, and can take alternative steps in monitoring a student:

I met with Ben on the corridor to ask about his welfare;
I observed him through his peer interactions and extra-curricular activities;
I spoke with his teachers about his class participation;
I remained in contact with his parents to determine his progress.

Undertaking these steps reassured me he was settling into a happier school life.

I feel the six weeks we worked together, gave him the skills he needed at the time. He knows there is a safe place that he can revisit if the need arises. He is going into transition year soon, a year that will offer new possibilities, friendships and challenges. For students like Ben it can be an extremely positive year and will allow him the chance to develop socially and personally.

Reflection...

For most teenagers, school is a place where learning occurs in a safe and secure atmosphere. But for some, it can be a place of intimidation, exclusion and torment. We now live in a society where bullying has taken on a whole new dimension, with the introduction of cyber-bullying and a notable increase in racism. We all know bullies and we all know victims. Many victims often feel powerless. But the greatest defence we can offer is to speak out and to ensure that aggressive and threatening behaviour is not tolerated. It is not acceptable to stand by and watch others being victimised, or to brush it off as a part of growing up. Making someone else uncomfortable, tormenting them or causing pain should never be tolerated. Parents, teachers, students and schools must endeavour to do two things:

1. To make it clear that bullying will not be tolerated in the community;

2. To create an environment in which the individual is not afraid to speak out.

I also work with students who bully. The bully needs counselling too. Often the bully acts out of a need. The reasons they do so are numerous. They may include:

Satisfying a need to express an underlying anger;
Wanting to belong;
Satisfying a need to be in control;
Wanting to hide insecurities e.g. low self-esteem;
Hoping to gain attention, not received elsewhere;
Acting out learned behaviour.

In order for a bully's behaviour to be remediated the Guidance Counsellor must counsel him or her as they would any student. It is only by resolving the bully's underlying problem, that the behaviour will cease. It is to help the 'bully' develop healthier ways to satisfy their needs and to take responsibility for their actions. Many do not intend to be so cruel and often lack the empathy or maturity to recognize the consequences of their behaviour. Encouraging involvement in sport, teaching new behaviours and allowing them space to talk all help the student in their development. My role and that of the whole school is to encourage positive behaviour.

Final Thought:

Signs are significant in counselling. Often, the unsaid is more indicative than what is spoken about. Therefore, the counsellor must really look and listen in order to really see and hear.

FOR STUDENTS

Tell an adult you can trust. Talking is your greatest weapon against bullying. You are never alone.
Do not suffer in silence.
Write out your own account of what has been happening.
Where possible walk away from a threatening situation.
Protect yourself from violence and aggression.
Try not to react-bullies love reactions.
Make friends with others who are on their own.
Don't believe what the bully says about you. The bully is the problem, not you.
With cyber bullying 'SIBR IT': **S**ave it, **I**gnore it, **B**lock it, **R**eport it, **I**dentify it and **T**alk

FOR PARENTS

Stay calm, try not to over-react.
Communicate: hear what is said and be aware of the signs.
Make contact with the school.
Encourage positive self-awareness.
Encourage involvement in extra-curricular activities.
Where physical bullying occurs outside school report it to the Gardaí.
Monitor and limit the use of the internet.

FOR THE PASTORAL TEAM

Deal with the situation calmly.
Always deal with it outside of the classroom.
Keep a written account of any incident.
When interviewing the victim and bully separately, get a written report of their own account of events.
Follow the school's Policy on Bullying.
Explain the limits of confidentiality

Further Information...

Useful Websites

www.bully4u.ie

Bully4u provides anti-bullying services for both primary and secondary schools, such as, bullying and cyber bullying workshops, presentations to parents and in-service for teachers.

www.schooldays.ie/articles/bullying

Schooldays.ie is an online resource for parents and teachers covering topics from health and well-being and bullying issues.

www4.dcu.ie/abc

The Anti-Bullying Research and Resource Centre (ABC), is based in Dublin City University. It also provides resources and training to those who wish to address the issue of bullying in schools.

www.ispcc.ie

Irish Society for the Prevention of Cruelty to Children (ISPCC) offer a number of online supports for those who are affected by bullying.

-        Online Bullying Support Service for children and young people.

-        TEXT: Text 'Bully' to 50101

-        A one-to-one live web-chat available on www.childline.ie

         Helpline: 1800 66 66 66 (24 hours a day)

Suggested Reading

Brian Lennon's Cool Anger Management Programme (CAM) offers a series of activities to help teenagers deal with strong emotions.

Available to download on:
(portal.meathvec.ie/schools/.../Cool%20Anger%20Management.pdf)
Brian Lennon is a Guidance Counsellor and Psychologist.

Chapter 5
Coming Out

Tulip
Every garden is enriched by the variety and colour offered by the tulip.

Coming Out

The question of sexuality and sex orientation is a relatively new area for me to work in, as a Counsellor. It is only in the last ten years, with the liberalising of our society that the issue has been raised more regularly. Up until about five years ago, it had never been a reason for a student to come to see me. Or, maybe it was, but was never voiced. In today's world students are more aware of what it is to be gay, lesbian or bisexual. Television series such as 'GLEE' and 'Mrs. Brown's Boys' and chat show hosts like Ellen DeGeneres have all helped to break down stereotypes and the misinformation about being gay. They have all encouraged people to express their true feelings and identity.

School can be a tough enough place for young people, without also feeling isolated and being bullied or ridiculed because they are gay. It is quite normal to feel confused and unsure of where your attractions lie.

'Coming out', while still in school, is very much a personal decision. Some choose to make it very public and tell everyone, some tell only those closest to them and others keep it to themselves. 'Bottling it up' will only lead to unhappiness and serious difficulties later on in life.

For parents that have a son or daughter who comes out there are many concerns and questions:

Is he just going through a phase?
Will he get over it?
She's only a child, how does she know if she's gay?
Can I do anything to change her mind?
How will this change his life?

These concerns are very real and it can take many years before a parent will accept it as a reality. The whole question of identity, whether it is sexual or social, is complex and diverse. It is influenced by a myriad of factors. There is no defined set of social, economic, cultural, ethnic or other factors that determine sexual identity. It is not a choice that one makes. It is part of who a person is.

The three accounts that follow, express the everyday realities faced by some students who are gay. All three, were mature, articulate and discreet students, which is reflected in their writing. I hope that through their words, some of the questions will be answered.

Introducing Michael... Aged 15...

I met Michael towards the end of third year. He was an extremely pleasant and intelligent young man. He was articulate and spoke in a gentle and sincere manner. He stopped by the office one day to ask if he could have a chat. He was nervous and fidgety when he sat down first, not knowing where to start. He said he thought that he was gay. He admitted it was something he had been thinking about for a long time and needed to tell someone. Michael spoke openly. He had felt 'different' for the past few years. He was able to identify certain things in his life that raised questions, for him, about his sexuality. He knew he was not attracted to girls. He felt certain of that.

The Approach I Used...

The most critical approach I used with Michael was to act as a sounding-board and mirror for him. It was to listen. Through simply listening I provided the opportunity for him to unfold. I acted almost as a passive agent, allowing Michael to voice his truths. I felt that he needed to have his story heard and responded to positively and without judgement. Implicit in this approach was acceptance of him.

As the appointment evolved, his shoulders relaxed, he regained eye contact and the fidgeting lessened.

We spoke about who he would like to tell and what their responses might be. We spoke about telling his parents and the reaction he might encounter. He decided that he would tell his close friends first. He would need their support. I encouraged him to take his time. He had kept these thoughts and feelings inside for so long, that the relief of saying it aloud was a huge first step. It might take others, particularly his parents, time to adjust.

He left the office that day, more confident, reassured and with his own plan of how he would take the next step. I had assured him of confidentiality as I did not believe him to be a student at risk. I also referred him to additional online support services available should it be required and left the option open for him to return.

Michael's Story... His own account.

I am a boy and I like girls. I also like boys. Confused? I was too. I didn't know who or what I liked. I had been in relationships with girls before and quite enjoyed them. But I had always looked at guys, checking out their appearances and physiques, it was attraction. I used to brush these feelings for men aside and try to forget them, acting almost as if they were wrong. Then I began to think and create an array of theories trying to justify how I felt, rationalising my feelings. It wasn't until much later that I finally felt able to accept myself. Even at that point I had doubts. I was afraid that the whole LGBT (Lesbian Gay Bisexual and Transgender) culture and ideal was appealing to me too much, and that I just wanted to be part of it all. It was after much more thinking that I became comfortable with my feelings and felt the need to tell people.

I never really thought of all this as 'coming out', more expressing how I feel. I was so nervous at the prospect that the person I turned to was the school Guidance Counsellor. The relief of telling someone what I had bottled up for so long was immense. After the advice and help of this lovely lady I proceeded to tell two friends. I was met with a mixture of huge support and indifference. My nerves had been for nothing. The thing is, and it took time for me to see, is that it doesn't change you. Your whole life doesn't change before your very eyes, you haven't transformed, you're still you!

All this worry and fear had developed during third year. Transition year changed all this for me. I made some truly amazing friends. I became comfortable and established myself. People knew who I was. I wanted to go into TY as a normal person, the same as everyone else. I didn't want to be labelled as a 'queer' or a 'faggot', judged before people even spoke to me. I wanted things my way.

My biggest fear was telling my family, the people I live with and know longest. I really didn't know where to begin. No-one had ever expressed any opinion on LGBT issues.

I was petrified. To this date, I have only told my mum, this was a lengthy process and we still don't see eye to eye on it. When I first told her in third year, she felt I was confused because I was under a lot of pressure with exams and wasn't mixing a whole lot. This kind of made sense at the time so I left it and waited. I brought up the subject again about a year later.

She believes it is a huge statement for someone so young and that I should conform and wait for college, for me to explore my feelings when I am older. But I don't want to wait and do not wish to conform. That's not to say I want to tell everyone, I just want to tell those closest to me.

In the long term I plan to leave Ireland and go somewhere like London or Berlin where anyone can be anything they wish. Ireland, I feel is narrow minded. I don't hold my mum personally responsible. Ireland was a very staunch Catholic country. Homosexuality was only decriminalised in 1993, but I'm still disheartened. I hope things change. Maybe she just needs more time to get used to it all. Time will tell. I just find it all oppressive.

TV shows such as Skins and Glee are dealing with sexuality and sexual confusion. They are raising awareness and helping it to become 'the norm'. Your teenage years are supposed to be the best years of your life, you discover who you are. Don't bottle things up, nothing should be taboo. If you are confused just take your time to think about things, don't just tell everyone and anyone. Friends should come first, at least then you'll have someone to fall back on after you tell your parents. By the way, your family will always love you, they might just need time to get used to things. There's no magic solution that will give you clarity and banish all of your troubles. No matter how confused or upset you may be, just think, talk and try to stick it out. You can't expect others to accept you if you can't accept yourself. No-one's looking for an answer straight away though. And at the end of the day - it's not who you are attracted to but who you fall in love with.

The Follow Up...

Each individual experience of 'Coming Out' is framed by a number of factors. These include the home and social context, the person's maturity / self-esteem and the support available. The availability of a safe, confidential and non-judgemental counselling service within the school afforded Michael the chance to speak openly.

There are three distinct stages in 'Coming Out':

Stage 1: Questioning – Michael experienced this primary phase over a period of years. It coincided with puberty: a time during which all adolescents question and attempt to make sense of their emerging sexual identity. They are driven by the need to experiment, explore and discover. It can be a time that is confusing and frightening. However, through 'Questioning', clarity is realised.

Stage 2: Accepting – For many students, acceptance begins with admission. Michael began to accept that he was gay when he shared his thoughts with others. His coming out to friends and family that year did more for him than he could have anticipated. He 'came out' of himself. With acceptance, the confusion lifted as he began to live truthfully and not secretively.

Stage 3: Integrating – Michael has now entered the stage of same-sex relationships. He has become more comfortable with his identity and the support offered by the LGBT community. He educated himself through the resources available to him and he took his time. His friends were a huge support to him during this time. His mother's reaction was cautious: she feared for him, but supported him.

Michael is a wise young man, popular among his peers and teachers alike. It may be a difficult road, but he has the skills to cope with the challenges ahead. He has the ability to do well in life because of the person he is, an educated and positive young man.

Introducing Leah.. Aged 15...

I had worked with Leah a long time before she told me that she was gay. Her parents had separated when she was in second year and her world changed dramatically. She had always been the girl that everyone looked up to, that everyone turned to for help and advice. She was a strong character, both caring and sensible. She was always top of the class, the 'minder' of the group and older than her years. She stood out among her peers for her maturity and sensitivity to others. When her parents separated, she withdrew into herself, missed school and lost all motivation for schoolwork. It was frustrating to watch such a good student change so rapidly.

Amidst this family disruption, other questions of identity were arising for Leah. We broached these questions together and it allowed Leah to admit to herself that she was gay. She confided she was attracted to girls. She had told her close friends and her mother, all of whom were extremely supportive. But it was a lot to carry on her young shoulders. She struggled more and more with attending school. Her greatest difficulty was that she felt she was now an adult. She felt she should be able to live the life of young gay woman, independent from her parents and her friends.

The Approach I Used...

Leah's situation was quite complicated. There were three key issues that needed to be addressed: absenteeism, a significant disruption in her home circumstances and a question over her sexual identity.

Leah's life was disjointed and dysfunctional. There was no structure or boundaries. Without these, no progress could be made. Leah understood that in order to regain control she needed to start attending school. With this in mind, we adjusted her timetable to facilitate re-engagement in school, giving her the platform from which she could rebuild.

She began to realise that school could provide her with the stability and consistency that was lacking in her home life. Once she settled into a routine in school she began to adjust to her new living arrangements also. This in turn, allowed us to explore her 'coming out' as the primary issue.

Leah's Story... Her own account.

I was 14 going on 15 when I first realised I was gay. I had never felt comfortable being with a boy, even holding a boy's hand would make me feel awkward or uncomfortable. It had never occurred to me that I might like girls. I wasn't trying to deny it to myself, I just never thought about it.

It first occurred to me one evening when I was with my best friend. He was gay. He asked me to go to a gay bar with him because he didn't want to go alone. So I said of course I'd go with him because I had always been supportive of his decision.

I was expecting nothing but to have a good night and that would be that. But while we were in there a girl came up to me and we chatted for the night and ended up exchanging numbers. We met a week later and I wasn't really sure what to expect or what I was doing. But we got together and I thought to myself, "I don't feel uncomfortable at all". Everything felt right. And that's how and when I knew I was gay.

I didn't tell any of my friends or my mum for about two months after. I think I just wanted to make sure this is what I wanted. Eventually I had made great friends and it was time to tell mum. She was very supportive and was always there for help. I didn't tell my Dad or the rest of the family till Christmas a year later. I was afraid of how he might react but it was who I was and he could either accept it or not.

I am so glad to this day that I had the courage to come out. Sometimes I feel very lonely thinking about the future because it isn't straight forward like a straight person's life. The norm is to go to college, fall in love with the right guy, get married and build the rest of your life together. But it can be very different for a gay person. The scene can be very bitchy, but you just have to ignore it and find out who your real friends are.

Thankfully I have found my true friends, although there have been bumps along the way. But I cannot stress enough how worth it, it is. It's important because you find out so many things about yourself and it makes you a better person.

Not a day goes by that I regret my decision, because it's me. What you see is what you get. My advice is just to always be yourself, never change for anyone and always remember you are never on your own.

Leah struggled with her Leaving Certificate. She dropped most of her subjects to ordinary level, despite having ability and potential. It was a very tough time for her. Coping with her parent's separation and finding her own identity at the same time, was a battle.

After school, Leah moved into her own place and began a new relationship. She continued to lack focus and direction. She dropped out of college and tried several different jobs. She was still very unsettled.

It can often take several years and life experiences, before a person finds a comfort zone, that allows them to accept themselves. In Leah's case she made the decision to return to college. This was a decisive step. It gave her a goal and her self-esteem benefitted. Building on this renewed self-esteem, she gave herself permission to be who she wanted to be, more confident and assured of her identity.

Introducing Dylan... Aged 18...

Dylan's 'coming out' was not an event. Instead, it was something that emerged as he grew. Dylan was unique, in that he never doubted his homosexuality. He was sure, comfortable and fully at ease within himself. It was a natural emergence of who he was. He did not attend counselling inside or outside school.

I knew Dylan and felt that his words could give advice to other students going through something similar. He always appeared happy, surrounded by friends, male and female. He was always involved in extra-curricular events, an area in which he is extremely talented. Other students admired him for this and judged him on his abilities rather than his sexuality.

Dylan's Story...

My couple of years in this secondary school, I can honestly say were the best in my life so far. It has one of the most welcoming, diverse, forward thinking communities of young people that I have ever come across. That is why I found it so easy to be gay.

When I look back over my time in school, I can't say there was a specific time where I stood up and made an announcement that I was gay. It was more about being myself around people, not hiding or lying. I never denied my sexuality, I let people come to me and ask me rather than shoving it in people's face. Everyone deals with this differently. Some people may prefer to tell everyone at once, others may wait until they have a partner to tell people. 'Coming out' is a process that can take someone's whole life.

For instance, I told my mum I was gay when I was fifteen, some might say this is very young to be really sure, but to them I say, when did you know you were straight? Is there ever the perfect time? There are both negatives and positives to coming out at that age. Some parents might not take it seriously because of your age. On the other hand it gives parents a chance to deal with it their own way and a few years down the line maybe things will then be fine.

Being out in school, being out in the big bad world for a few years, the next major hurdle for me in the 'coming out' process was having a boyfriend! It is surprisingly difficult introducing a guy to your family, even if they already know you are gay! It is great to be able to be at home with all the people you love around you and for everything to be 'normal'. I firmly believe that we, as gay people, are the main obstacle in us coming out.

We always assume it is going to be hard, that people won't accept us, that our lives are going to be full of discrimination and hatred. When most people find that when you take the first step of many it is indeed the road to a happy life, a life where you can be yourself, where the majority of people love you for who you are and not who you love. I understand that not everyone's stories are that easy, and many people are met with negativity when they come out. To those people I say never give up, be yourself and be comfortable being yourself. Being gay is not a choice, why would anyone choose a life that can be so difficult for some people?

Do not be afraid of what is to come. At the end of the day, nothing changes. You are still the person your family and friends know, they just now will know you better.

I am going to finish with a quote from Harvey Fierstien, An American playwright and actor. I think this is a good motto to live by:

'Never be bullied into silence. Never allow yourself to be made a victim. Accept no one's definition of your life. Define yourself.'

The Follow Up...

Dylan was lucky. He had a very supportive family who accepted him for who he was. He is a very well-adjusted and happy young man. I have no doubt that he may meet negative comments but his outlook on life is positive and encouraging.

He has found a niche for himself in the world of stage and drama and lives by his motto and defines himself. I have met a number of homosexual students whose ambition it is to be on stage. There is a tendency for them to gravitate to the Arts as it is perceived as a more welcoming forum in which to express themselves.

Reflection...

Unfortunately, in society there still exists stigma, taboo and prejudice regarding homosexuality. The younger generation is more accepting of differences and of the right we all have to free expression. Young people are more informed and educated about choices and possibilities open to them. As a result, it is likely that as Guidance Counsellors we will continue to meet more students who have questions about their own sexuality and identity. We will meet students who are extremely vulnerable and afraid to be seen as different. Some may face homophobic bullying, isolation and rejection, which can have a detrimental and damaging effect on their mental health. Coinciding with puberty and social, vocational and emotional development, it can be a very stressful time for students to 'come out'.

The Role of Schools:

Schools provide the context in which equality, justice, rights, responsibilities and a deep sense of community create the foundations of good citizenship and a healthy society. These goals are met through curriculum, policies, model behaviour and extra-curricular opportunities.

However, just as important as these formal strategies are the ethos, language and relationships observed by students. The aspiration to create a warm, safe and encouraging school context must be a lived reality. Students who witness and experience a fair and non-judgemental school life will accept it as the norm and carry this into their wider communities.

How do we translate this aspiration into a reality?

These objectives must be embedded in the school culture;

The language and action of the school must be unambiguous;

Tolerance and acceptance must be audible in formal and informal communication;

The subject of homosexuality must be presented as one congruent with the fight against racism and gender discrimination or stereotype.

There are obstacles and objectives:

Obstacles: **Objectives:**

Fear   Respect
Culture   Inclusivity
Attitude   Tolerance
Lack of Understanding   Acceptance
Discord   Social Growth
Machismo   Cultural Awareness
Labelling   Equality
Stereotypes   Justice
Resistance   Rights

Schools must be proactive in promoting programmes and initiatives that encourage the respect and freedom for diversity of all students. These programmes must also counter unacceptable language and behaviour.

Relationship and Sexuality Education (RSE)
Social, Personal and Health Education (SPHE)
Religious Education (RE)
Civic, Social and Political Education (CSPE)

It is now mandatory for all schools to have anti-bullying policies that include homophobic bullying.

An important point to remember is that underage sex, under the age of seventeen, for boys and girls, whether gay or straight, is illegal in Ireland.

It is imperative that any individual working with young people is aware and familiar with the new mandatory reporting procedures in relation to student welfare.

Final Thought:

Every counsellor is aware of the vulnerability of the students in their care. Therefore, the welfare of the student is at all times assessed and considered accordingly.

Guidance on Dealing with Coming Out...

FOR STUDENTS

Be proud of who you are.
In the early stages tell close friends you trust.
Remember there is nothing wrong with you because you are gay.
Check out websites and other resources to explore issues.
It takes courage to come out, take your time.
Remember, being gay is just a part of who you are, it doesn't define you.
Do talk to an adult if you are being bullied or feeling down.

FOR PARENTS

Take time to come to terms with learning that your son/daughter is gay.
Talk to someone you trust about your fears and concerns.
It is okay to feel sad, angry or worried.
Try not to suppress how you feel, it won't go away.
When you are ready, talk with your son/daughter about how you both feel.
Continue to give support. It will make a huge difference to their life.

FOR THE PASTORAL TEAM

Steps must be taken to prevent homophobic bullying in schools, through the school's anti-bullying policy.
If the student is under the age of consent, *Child Protection Guidelines* must be followed.
Always offer non-judgemental support.
Provide information on resources and support available.
Encourage self-acceptance.
Encourage peer support.
Always focus on the student and their needs.
Ensure that sexual orientation is referred to positively through SPHE and CSPE Programmes.

Further Information...

Useful Websites:

www.belongto.org

The **Belong To** Youth Service provides services, resources and information for LGBT young people and their parents.

www.teni.ie

TENI is the Transgender Equality Network Ireland, which aims to improve the conditions and rights of Transgender people.

National LGBT Helpline: 1890 929 539

The LGBT Helpline is confidential and non-judgmental. It provides listening, support and information for:

Lesbian, gay, bisexual and transgender (LGBT) people;
Their family and friends;
Those who are questioning if they might be LGBT.

www.glen.ie

Gay and Lesbian Equality Network (GLEN) aims to bring positive change for lesbian, gay and bisexual people in Ireland, focusing on equality and inclusion.

Suggested Reading

Each school has access to very useful information booklets and resources which have been compiled by the Department of Education and Science, the Health Service Executive and groups such as GLEN and BelongTo Youth Service.

For example:

Lesbian, Gay and Bisexual Students in Post-Primary Schools. Guidance for Principals and School Leaders. (DES)

Supporting LGBT Lives: A Study of the Mental Health and Well-being of Lesbian, Gay, Bisexual and Transgender People. (HSE)

Chapter 6
Depression

Bluebell
The common 'blue' of the forest thrives in shade, hidden from the light of open spaces.

Depression

We all have days when we feel down, when we find it difficult to peel ourselves out of bed, when we don't want to see other people or hold conversations. We all know what it is like to feel sad, to feel like crying and want to hide away from the world. This low mood, affects us all at some point in our lives. It might last an hour, a day, even a few days. But it passes, and we know it will pass, so we work through it.

Frequently, I meet students who present for counselling, because they are experiencing a low mood. In most cases they know why. For some, difficult days become weeks, sadness lingers and they struggle with understanding the reasons why. They might be experiencing some or all of the following symptoms:

Possible Signs of Depression to Look Out For:

Crying all the time and for no obvious reason

Finding it hard to get to sleep or stay asleep

Diminishing appetite or comfort eating

Lacking motivation for school or homework

Lacking concentration

Dropping out of extra-curricular activities

Becoming more irritable or angry

Feeling lonely even when with their friends

Feeling worthless

Feeling tired all the time

Suffering headaches or stomach aches

It is always important to rule out any underlying medical condition as soon as possible, by referring the student to a GP.

Introducing Michelle... Aged 17...

To all who knew her, Michelle was outgoing, confident, chatty and sociable. She was an excellent student and loved to be involved in a whole range of projects. She really enjoyed school and participated enthusiastically. She had a large group of friends and stood out as the one they all turned to if they had a problem. But this persona masked the real truth. Behind the smiles and the confidence was a very unhappy girl. She was confused, sad and even lonely at times, despite having friends. She couldn't explain these feelings. She had become a master at hiding them from family and friends. She portrayed two very different personalities depending on her situation; one that was extrovert, the other introvert.

The Approach I Used...

During the counselling appointments Michelle would talk freely. She could articulate very well the thoughts and emotions spinning around in her head. I encouraged her to write at night when she was restless and to pass on these letters to me if she wished. She wrote pages and pages to try and give life to these feelings. She was inquisitive, philosophical and introspective. Some of her thoughts centred on the meaning of life and the after-life. Some focused on her own life and what her future held:

I think about life, the point of it. What's it all for?
It's full of ups and downs and eventually you die. Then what?
What worries me now is the future. How do I change it?
What do I do?
Why is it that when my life is fine, I sometimes hate it?
Why do I find myself thinking about death and suicide?

All of this created a confused and exhausted troubled teenager. My first priority was to determine if Michelle was at risk of harming herself. Counselling is normally about using open questioning, allowing the student to speak freely. In certain instances questioning must be direct and to the point, in order to determine what action to take. I asked her:

Do you want to kill yourself?
Have you a plan?
How would your family react?

From her answers I was able to deduce that she did not want to take her own life by suicide but she found herself preoccupied with it. I still referred her to her GP who determined that she was suffering from depression. He prescribed medication, which she chose not to take and instead opted to continue attending counselling with me.

It was a very long process of listening and understanding, working through questions in detail. Her mind was always racing, always questioning, always full of self-doubt and over analysis.

In order to help Michelle cope with over thinking and negative thoughts about herself, I encouraged her to draw a diagram, with herself at the centre. I asked her to list all the issues that were getting her down. She wrote words like 'myself', 'family', 'friends', 'thoughts', 'worries' and 'school'. For each session we talked through how she felt about each one and the positive or negative each one brought to her life. Through her letters and poetry clarity began to emerge. The constant worrying began to lift as she gained control again of her thoughts and focused on dealing with one issue at a time.

Michelle wrote the following poem during the initial stages of the counselling process.

Life Within A Tear

I need you to imagine life within a tear
Enclosed by walls of water, like glass, so far but yet so near.
I need you to experience the feelings, ones of pain
Drowning in frustration, paranoia, hurt and shame.
People see you through this wall of glass
To them you're distant but you're there.
They come so close, you try reach out,
But they forget, pull back, don't seem to care.
You do get tired of endless struggles
Friendships, plans... they fall apart,
And all this feeling mounts inside you
It fills your mind, then fills your heart.

And then at times you crave release,
You crack and pray for it to end,
And then at times you feel alone
And then you pray for just a friend.
Afraid to knock the wall you built
To reach beyond and grab the hands
You fear the hands will leave you go
That they'll give up, not understand.
I fight things on my own,
It's the only way I learned to cope,
Maybe someone will teach me new ways
And while I wait, I live in hope.

The Follow Up...

After months of support and learning new ways to lift her mood and calm her mind, Michelle began to understand the endless insecurities and questions of *Why? What if? How? When?* Her questioning all seemed to stem from *Who am I?* It was more about her identity and feeling happy in her own skin. She had realised that being the friend who everyone turned to was, at times, overwhelming, and brought out her own uncertainties.

After school, and having completed her degree, Michelle found her niche and settled into a stable and rewarding career. When I now meet her, I still see the confident young woman she portrayed in school. I often wonder though, does she still question so much and battle with the need for definite answers? Is she now happy with the person she is? Has she accepted it?

Introducing Katie... Aged 17...

I had known Katie as a hard-working, polite and enthusiastic student, with a flair for art and an eagerness to help others. She was an excellent student with a desire to achieve. During a guidance appointment she spoke of her goal to study medicine and become a doctor. She met with me concerned that her grades did not match her ambition. The realisation that she might not achieve her goal seemed to trigger a blow to her self-esteem and to the wall of confidence she portrayed. It was important for us to address the emotional and esteem issues arising from the gap between her grades and her dreams. This cause of concern had depressed her. It had led to a prolonged 'low' that we needed to explore.

The Approach I Used...

My first task was to teach Katie two strategies to help her lift her mood. Over the next two weeks we concentrated on how she was thinking. When we are in a low mood we tend to have only negative thoughts.

1.   Positive Thinking:

Each day she made a list of three negative thoughts she had, and reshaped them into challenges she could overcome. Instead of Katie saying I can't do this or I will never achieve my goal now, I wanted her to turn these statements into positive ones. I can do this and I will do my best.

2.   Positive Actions:

She also listed three small tasks to accomplish each day. For example:

Going for a walk;
Taking a bath;
Organising her bedroom.

Compounded by the stress of exams approaching, Katie struggled to achieve these goals. Conscious of a two week break coming up, I referred her to her GP and to a Cognitive Behavioural Therapist, as I felt she would need continued support outside of school.

Katie's Story... written as an 18-year-old...

I started feeling down last summer. I applied pressure to myself - big time. I am a perfectionist and I used to always think getting good grades was so important. I had everything; good grades, a life ambition to become a doctor, a large group of friends, a part-time job and a boyfriend. But I wasn't happy on the inside. I tried to confide in my best friend but she was fed up of me complaining. I was depressed. The next three months were the worst of my life. Between fights with my friends and boyfriend, I was a wreck. I was drifting further away from everyone. The stress of school and staying to the standard I saw fit was unbearable.

I decided to visit the Guidance Counsellor to discuss my future. We went through the possibility of me getting the high points and determined that it was unlikely. Being in such a dark place, this news hit me hard. I was devastated. My boyfriend then broke up with me. My whole world crashed around me. Everything I had bottled up came out. I didn't want to be here. I wanted to fall asleep and never wake up.

That was the beginning. I went back to the Guidance Counsellor to explain my suicidal thoughts. It was so hard. I still didn't want to believe even then that I was depressed. She referred me onto my GP. After a few visits he put me on anti - depressants. I was deteriorating quickly. My exams were a disaster and I didn't want to get out of bed. I was miserable. I felt constant nausea from the medication. I hit rock bottom. I took an overdose of painkillers - not a good idea! I ended up in A&E, having blood tests and a vigorous psychological analysis. It was the scariest thing I have ever been through.

I had to deal with Suicide Counselling, Cognitive Behavioural Therapy and numerous doctor appointments. It was so hard. My mum was my rock and she pulled me through it. My ex-boyfriend was too, he is now one of my best friends. But I got through it. I have a whole new group of friends and things are so much better now. I have decided to study Art instead and become an Art teacher. I am so happy now. Don't get me wrong I still have my bad days and I cry, but that's depression isn't it?

Depression isn't a thing to be ashamed of. I was once, but now I am not. I don't openly broadcast my depression but I am not afraid. I realise now that it was a blessing in disguise. My life is so much better now. I got through it and I am so proud of myself. Life isn't easy but it's so important not to give up. When I was at my lowest it was hard to hear people say it will get better, it will be ok. But take it from me, it does get better. With help from others, I have learnt it will be ok.

The Follow Up...

Katie's low mood had developed slowly over the previous six months but once she voiced it, things began to escalate. She found herself fighting depression and anxiety. We made the decision, along with her doctor, that she would take some time off from school to get herself back in a routine. After several tough weeks of Cognitive Behavioural Therapy and medication changes, things began to settle down and Katie's mood lifted.

She returned to school the following year, attended regularly and found a new group of friends. She has now finished the counselling sessions and for the moment, remains on medication. She has looked at other possible career options and has made more realistic goals.

Introducing Sophie... Aged 14...

Sophie was a 14-year-old girl who had regular nightmares. They were terrifying and shocking. She could vividly recall scenes of destruction and devastation. The same theme recurred night after night, with the same characters involved. She felt threatened and scared. She was afraid to go to sleep. Initially, I wondered if this was just the mind of a very creative teenager who had read too many 'Twilight' novels or watched too much 'CSI' before going to bed. But with the nightmares came other symptoms; headaches, loss of motivation and concentration and anger.

The nightmares worsened and Sophie began to hear voices telling her to harm herself. She was now living a nightmare.

The Approach I Used...

To discover the source of the nightmares I encouraged Sophie to draw pictures, to illustrate the story occurring in her dreams. She was a keen artist and expressed herself best through her drawings. With each appointment the drawings became darker and more sinister. The characters started to come to life around her. On several occasions she spoke about these characters being in the room with her. When this occurred, her body became rigid and her face conveyed panic. When a student is in such a heightened state, it is important to concentrate on breathing and calming techniques. The Ground, Breathe, Think (GBT) Approach works best in these scenarios.

In Sophie's case I knew further intervention was needed when the nightmares and headaches became relentless. I also noticed that beneath the bangles and bracelets she wore on her wrists, lay another cry for help. Sophie had been cutting herself – she was self-harming. I immediately contacted her parents and an emergency appointment was made with her GP. He referred her to the local Child and Adolescent Mental Health Services (CAMHS). Sophie and her family went through a very anxious time. She underwent medical investigations to try to determine the cause of the headaches, but all tests came back clear. She attended a psychiatrist with CAMHS over the next few months and was eventually diagnosed with depression. Typically, these appointments with psychiatrists were every two weeks and often they were with different psychiatrists.

Written after several months of counselling.

I don't belong here, I don't deserve to be here,
I don't have a place here, I don't even know why I'm here,
I don't even enjoy being here, I don't want to be the freak here,
I don't want my troubles out here, I don't want to be here!

These are a few of the thousands of things that were on replay in my head. I couldn't think of anything else besides being dead. Since then I have learnt more than enough, and guess what?! I'm finally...FREE. I found my way and unlocked the cage of unhappiness, darkness and loneliness with help, support and the ounce of willpower I had left in my tired and sore body. I found the key!

I know I wasn't myself before, but now, I am. I am so grateful to my family but also to everyone else. Without their constant support and unlimited love I wouldn't be here now, writing this. I still believe that I didn't deserve all the stuff they did for me, all the money they spent to get me the best that money could buy. But now, I am better and am slowly starting to see how much they truly love me and would do anything for me to be safe and happy.

I'm starting to believe! I won't lie, I still have my down days and yes, I feel like punching a wall but that punch to the wall is better than a knife to the skin.

I AM BETTER, I AM STRONGER! So when I have those days, I keep my head held high, smile on my face and I tell those bad thoughts that they cannot control me anymore.

If you find yourself in a bad place, don't keep it to yourself, tell someone you trust and accept the help. Once you do and WHEN you get through your difficult stage, you will be saying what is on replay in my head day to day now.

I belong here, I am loved here.
I have hope here, I fit in here.
I have people who care about me here. I have a right to be here,
I am happy here. I am thankful for being here,
I HAVE A FUTURE HERE!

The Follow Up...

A number of procedures were put in place to assist Sophie's senior years in school:

1.   I asked the Special Needs Department to investigate if Sophie had an underlying learning difficulty which may have added to her stress. They diagnosed her with a Specific Learning Difficulty. She received one-to-one resource hours and learning support. This helped in maintaining concentration and reducing her headaches.

2.   Her timetable was reduced to allow her more time for certain subjects.

3.   As her appointments with the psychiatrist were sporadic, I suggested that she attend Art Therapy. For artistic students it is a rewarding method of expressing and understanding emotions. It would also offer her consistency and security.

Over time her nightmares began to disappear and she became more settled and less frustrated. She successfully completed her Leaving Certificate and chose a career path suited to her practical mind and her creative talents.

A high proportion of students attending counselling present with symptoms of depression. It is often the first physical sign that there is something wrong. It might appear as being over tired, run down, withdrawn, sad or unmotivated. It usually develops over a period of weeks and the student feels stuck and unable to free themselves of the negative feelings. This is very different to a low mood which passes in a few days. Depression is debilitating. It takes away our sense of control and contentment. It becomes exhausting. Even the simplest of tasks can appear unachievable.

The first step in treating depression is through talking. It can be a very slow process and is often compounded by many other factors. Sometimes the cause is not easily identifiable and so it may take a few weeks before the student begins to feel some 'normality' again.

The following sample tasks can be useful to focus the student and encourage positive thinking:

Listing all the symptoms / feelings at present;
Listing their goals, no matter how small;
Introducing daily tasks e.g. organise room;
Encouraging them to keep a journal;
'Pay it forward' and do something nice for someone else.

The second step is to encourage exercise. Any form of exercise, walking, running or cycling. Often when a student is depressed they don't feel like taking part in team sports as their energy is too low and they retreat socially into themselves. Even half an hour a day will make a big difference.

The use of medication in treating depression may sometimes be a necessity. In cases where there is no improvement in symptoms and if there is any cause for concern for the student's mental health it is vital to refer them on to their GP. In most instances it is a temporary measure used for a couple of months until there has been an improvement and the person is ready to move forward.

Final Thought:

Counselling allows for unfolding to take place. Unfolding, takes time, attention and focus. Time to listen, time to discover, time to learn and time to rebuild.

Guidance on Dealing with Depression...

FOR STUDENTS

Talk to someone.
Give yourself small goals to achieve each day.
Make sure to treat yourself when you achieve these goals.
Instead of saying 'I can't' say 'I can'.
Keep a diary – write how you feel each day.
Go for a walk – it will help a lot.
Know that this feeling WILL pass.

FOR PARENTS

Always rule out medical conditions - make an appointment with your GP,
who will refer your son / daughter to the appropriate services if needed.
Be patient.
Encourage talking – if not to you, then to another adult.
Praise success in managing tasks and achievements.
Encourage involvement in hobbies and interests.
Let them know they can get through it.

FOR THE PASTORAL TEAM

Talk with the student if you have concern.
Encourage the need for them to accept help.
Let them know that help is available.
If a student is considered at risk, follow the appropriate procedures of
referral necessary.
Document any concerns you might have.

Further Information...

Useful Websites

www.aware.ie

Aware offers information, education and support to those affected by depression, stress or mood disorders.

It delivers two educational programmes to secondary school students called **Beat the Blues** and **Life Skills** which trains students how to manage mild to moderate depression or anxiety.

Email: *supportmail@aware.ie*

The Aware Support Line 1890 303 302

www.mentalhealthireland.ie

Mental Health Ireland is a national voluntary organisation that provides information and training on issues of mental health.
It provides educational programmes such as:

1. The National Public Speaking Project for senior students in post-primary schools promotes an awareness of the importance of positive mental health;

2. Mental Health Matters, a mental health resource pack for students which addresses the issue of mental health in an age-appropriate manner.

www.letsomeoneknow.ie

Let Someone Know is a website for teenagers offering information, advice and support on the issue of mental health.

www.reachout.com

ReachOut.com is run by the Inspire Ireland Foundation which is a registered charity. It provides information on issues that affect mental health and well-being.

Chapter 7
Sexual Abuse

Fuchsia
The fuchsia becomes its true self, when it is ready to unfold.

Sexual Abuse

Students who have been sexually abused are often too frightened to disclose this fact straight away. Generally, they tend to present with a different problem to 'test' the trustworthiness of the counsellor. (Remember, the issue of trust, has been significantly broken.) Throughout the appointments, 'hints' can be thrown in to judge the counsellor's reaction. As a result it can take quite a while before a disclosure of abuse is made.

When this finally happens, the relief for some students can be immense; for others it can be terrifying. They may have been threatened into silence and forced to keep this secret to themselves for years. They may also be terrified that the news could be detrimental to their family.

In all of the sexual abuse cases that I have worked with, the abuser was known to the victim and was a family friend, neighbour or relative. The abuse is usually not confined to a single incident, but takes place over a considerable length of time.

There is never just one indicator or warning sign of abuse, but several. By the time the student has the courage to break their silence they will already be showing some or all of these signs.

Possible Signs of Sexual Abuse to Look Out For:

Appearing withdrawn or sad
Displaying unexplained aggression
Self-Harming
Being extremely irritable
Having difficulty making eye contact
Having difficulty making new friends
Needing constant affirmation from teachers
Exhibiting significant weight gain or weight loss
Expressing a reluctance to return home after school

It is important to note that this is not an exhaustive list and no one indicator should assume abuse.

The following case studies have been written by female students which may reflect the fact that male students may be less inclined to report abuse. They too are vulnerable and may be inhibited by confiding in a female counsellor. Already feeling emasculated they may also consider the disclosure, a negative reflection on their manhood.

Introducing Sarah... Aged 17...

Sarah was seventeen. I knew her to be a strong-minded, capable and independent girl. She returned to school after the summer break with a definite change in behaviour. She was withdrawn and did not appear to want to mix with others as she had before. According to her teachers, her classroom behaviour had also changed. She had always involved herself in class debates and discussions. But now she was quiet in class, opting not to participate. She had become aggressive and argumentative when asked for her opinions on issues. Sarah was referred to me for counselling.

Initially she was closed, defensive and sullen. Her mother made contact with me and informed me that Sarah had been abused that summer, by a relative. The abuse took place while Sarah and her family were visiting with relations. Her mother had made contact with the Gardaí and the circumstances were being investigated.

The Approach I Used...

In the months that followed we worked through her feelings of despair, hurt, guilt and sadness. During each session I concentrated on helping Sarah put words to her feelings. For this exercise I used Gem Stones; all different colours, sizes and designs. (Marbles can also be used.) When the student can hold, see and examine something tangible it removes their focus from the fear of talking. They begin to relax and open up. I then asked questions like:

Which one would you choose to describe how you are feeling right now?
Which one would you choose to describe the despair you feel?
What made you choose that one?
Which one would you choose to describe how you would like to feel?

I also encouraged Sarah to keep a diary and to write when she couldn't sleep or felt alone. Sometimes she would show me what she had written and we would discuss it. Gradually, her writing became less about despair and guilt and more about her strength and hope. The counselling provided Sarah with a place to talk and be heard and most importantly the chance to learn to trust another adult again.

The following are two early extracts from her diary:

Sarah's Story... Her diary entries:

The past few months haven't really been too good. When people ask me how things are I generally have a tendency to say "fine", whether that's what I wanted to say or not. At the time it seems easier to say that, but in the end it is worse. Things have a way of building themselves up.

I haven't been able to sleep with the light off lately and it really freaks me out. Bad dreams have become a bit more frequent. I think that's what caused the light thing, a bit too many dreams together. I woke up screaming at somebody to get out of my room. It was 2:30 am and everybody was asleep! I started shouting and hitting at someone who wasn't there. Then I woke up fully and thought "What am I doing?!" The room suddenly felt very dark around me and I felt someone might be there, though I knew no one was. I had to turn the light on straight away. That was nearly three weeks ago - I haven't been able to sleep with the light off since.

I don't know what to do. It's really been getting to me. During the day I just get on with things but at night... I don't know. I don't think I can deal with them too well so I just switch off. I do need to talk but I just don't know what to say.

Lights Out

Lights out
Nowhere to run
Fear and darkness stand alone.
Thoughts run deep
Emotions high
Need all the answers "Why?"

Why life so full of pain,
Then death
We've nothing to gain.
All this pain inside of me
Don't know what to do
Can't live this life,
Don't want to die,
Fear of the unknown.
Where to go to find the light,
What to do if I succeed.
Left to wander, left to wonder,
All alone with no one by my side.

The Follow Up...

It took a year to help Sarah find her self-confidence again. Through talking and writing she regained her self-esteem. She became empowered to take back the control she had lost.

Under extremely difficult circumstances Sarah took the very brave step of seeking justice. She made a decision that would change her life and turn a traumatic experience into something positive. She decided to pursue justice through the courts. She was already out of school by the time she made this decision, but she did return to me to get help writing her statement and preparing for court. It was extremely distressing for her to revisit that terrible night, but it was cathartic and liberating.

The case was heard and Sarah gave her evidence. Her abuser was found guilty and was given a prison sentence. It was the hardest path she could have chosen, but she was resilient. Counselling had given her the courage to pursue this path. She was ably guided by legal, professional and court liaison officers who enabled her to testify. In offering her story here, in these pages, she acts as a testament to how counselling and guidance can allow for a person to reassert themselves and begin again.

Most victims of sexual abuse do not seek justice legally. The process can be lengthy and humiliating. Most teenagers, at this stage in their development, are not emotionally equipped to cope with taking that step.

Introducing Rachel... Aged 16...

I met Rachel on a weekly basis for several months, dealing with issues of depression and addiction. During one appointment, she disclosed that she had been abused as a young child, by a man whom she knew and who is now deceased.

She had all the signs of having been violated as a young child. She was damaged both physically and emotionally. She felt guilty, ugly, worthless and confused. She struggled to deal with these emotions, which often became too much for her. She had carried this 'secret' for many years and finally found the courage to make her voice heard.

The Approach I Used...

I immediately informed the Principal of Rachel's disclosure. He then contacted her parents who informed him that they were aware of the abuse and had made the appropriate steps to handle it at the time. They were happy for me to continue working with her, as she had not spoken to another professional about it since and had locked it away. As she turned 16, and became more aware of herself, the trauma resurfaced. She knew she needed to talk.

I wanted her to trust that sharing the past with someone could help her heal. With each session, the trust grew. She felt comfortable, at ease and safe. My office and our weekly meetings provided her with a sense of security. The challenges we faced together as counsellor and client were many. The most damaging obstacle for Rachel was guilt. Most victims of sexual abuse harbour a sense of guilt, from which they cannot easily detach themselves. It was imperative that Rachel relinquished her guilt and transferred it to the man who was to blame, her abuser.

One thing that did help was writing. It gave her the freedom to express herself without judgement. This honesty allowed her to conquer her guilt and begin to rebuild her self-esteem.

Rachel's Story... Her own account:

Today I saw him again-he always says hi and I always look away. He must think I'm ignorant, but I don't know who's more ignorant at the end of it all. I just think, why? Was it my fault? Was it anybody's fault? My childhood memories go from playing on the road with my friends to being in a bedroom with him, his bedroom, that big dark spare room, the boy's room. I suppose in his eyes he was giving me a guided tour. I know he charged me for it anyway! I can just see him now standing at his front door...just like my Grandad I suppose. Maybe that's why I liked and trusted him, because my Grandad was my favourite person as a child. But then he, my neighbour, comes along with his horrible thoughts and gets his kicks off young kids.

I lie in bed at night and wonder what he used to think when he watched the news and saw that a girl had been raped or assaulted or whatever. Did he think "You Bastard!" or did he think "Fair play!"? What if someone abused his kids? Or did he abuse them?

Hate is too nice a term to convey what I feel for him. Just the thought of his hands touching me, stroking my hair, telling me it would be alright - What was going to be "all right" - I was five! I didn't have problems. Now it's not alright so why say it?

All over his house were pictures of his children so I'm guessing he loved them and was proud of them. And here he is with his sick little mind, touching me on one of their beds. Every time I think of him I get this tight twisted knot in my stomach, my hands shake and I honestly feel like throwing up. He's just disgusting!

Looking out of my bedroom window now I see about five or six young kids playing outside his house like I used to do with my friends and they are so happy in their innocence. In all the hatred and in all the anger I have inside me, I am eternally grateful that he is dead. Nobody should ever have to think the thoughts I do, or have to cry themselves to sleep, because of the dreams they have. I'm going to beat him. I'm going to beat this and if I can turn half of this hatred into positivity then I know I'll be alright.

I Think, I Cry, I Sleep

I think
I cry
I sleep
These are my days.
The past
The present
The future
These are my pains
The fear
The anger
The solitude
These are my feelings

So after my days,
my pains and my feelings
- what is left?
Will I succumb to this black desolate hole,
I've come to know and hope to overcome them?
Or do I lie down and die?
What is easier?
Confrontation with life?
Confrontation with death?

These are my choices.

The Follow Up...

If Rachel hadn't spoken of her childhood memories, I have no doubt that she would not be who she is today. Secondary school was not an easy place for her to be, while having to deal with such horrific memories. But it did offer her a place to heal. It was a turning point. A place where she could find support and have her story listened to. It took a long time, but this is where she is today, in her own words:

Thankfully I'm no longer that person but I think now I'm wise enough to know it's not that hard to find yourself back there. My new mantra and quite possibly the most powerful word in the dictionary is, 'Choice'.

I can happily report, that life does indeed find me well at the moment. I'm happy and I'm headed in pretty good directions. Live the life you have imagined.

Introducing Ciara... Aged 16...

Ciara was a bubbly, gentle and caring girl, who loved life and showed it. She came to me upset one day and asked if she could tell me something.

Ciara experienced an incident where she was sexually harassed in her own home by a neighbour. For a child, like Ciara, the event was shocking, frightening and confusing.

Ciara's Story... Her own account:

Mr. X was our neighbour. He visited our home regularly. I didn't think it was strange when he called me that Monday when my parents were out. He sat and chatted with me and joked as normal. He had brought me treats, thinking I'd be lonely when my parents were away.

Before I knew it he grabbed me and started kissing me. I couldn't stop him. I was in shock. I just froze. Was this really happening? Eventually I pushed him and ran into the hall. He followed me and tried to kiss me again.

I started to shout and call for help. He stopped then and said he would leave. I locked the front door to shut him out. I was so scared he would come back again.

The Approach I Used...

Two factors mitigated the impact on Ciara's well-being:

1.   Her prompt disclosure of the incident;

2.   The subsequent pro-active approaches of counselling, the Principal, parents and the Gardaí.

This meant that the actions of Ciara's network of support lessened the effect on her mental health.

When she told her story she was shaking and traumatised. I encouraged her to tell her parents about what had happened so that they could deal with it as a family and prevent it happening again. I also informed the Principal who met with her parents to take the appropriate next step. Knowing the person made the situation extremely difficult and delicate.

Ciara felt a huge sense of relief after talking. Even though she had not wanted her parents to know what had happened, a huge weight was lifted when she realized that they believed her.

During the few weeks that we met, I concentrated on how it made her feel and the effect it had on her self-esteem. For each negative comment like 'shame', 'guilt' and 'dirty', I asked Ciara to answer some questions:

What do you like about yourself?
What are your talents?
What words would your friends use to describe you?
What are your strengths?

I wanted her to become aware of all the positive things about herself and her life. I praised her assertive behaviour and how she had stood up to her abuser. When she was getting stronger I suggested that she write a letter of confrontation to her abuser. We practiced it a few times and discussed what she wanted to say. Through writing the following letter she found a way to express the anger and hurt that she felt towards him. It was a letter she never sent.

I hate you. I hate you. I hate you!
You terrified me. You ruined my life, my house, my home, my street, myself. They will never be the same. You are sick. You seriously need help. You are a pervert. I blamed myself for so long, thinking it was my fault. I hope you get what you deserve. Only people like you can get away with this horrible, creepy and sick stuff.
I don't want anyone to go through what you put me through. It was your fault, not mine!
I hate you!!

The Follow Up...

Ciara's parents made a complaint about the man that abused her. He received a warning from the Gardaí but the case never went any further. He no longer has any contact with the family.

Before the school broke for the summer holidays, I referred Ciara on for counselling to the Rape Crisis Centre which she attended for several weeks. Initially, she was slow to tell her story again. She had put everything into building trust with me as her counsellor and did not want to have to go through it all again with someone new.

This can be a huge difficulty for students when they are referred to another professional. I wanted Ciara to have support during the summer holidays. Referral to another professional is often necessary and is in the best interests of the student. The advantage is that they are more prepared than they think. They understand what is involved and they learn new ways of coping.

Ciara returned for her final year having regained a sense of self and with an air of maturity. She had lost some of her innocence and childish ways. Despite the negative experience she has remained a positive and bubbly young woman and has made a career in helping others.

Reflection...

Everyone hears the statistic that one in every four people will suffer sexual abuse at some point in their life. It is a very significant percentage. The number of students reporting sexual abuse to guidance counsellors has decreased over the years. This may be because the incidents are decreasing or that the students are afraid to report it, for fear of not being believed.

As with the case studies in this chapter, all situations differ greatly. In my experience few have gone to court, either because the abuser is deceased or the victim is not ready to cope with such an event. Where the abuser is a family member, many factors need to be taken into consideration. It is an extremely complex scenario that <u>always</u> needs professional advice and support to address the number of losses felt by the victim:

Loss of control;
Loss of self-respect;
Loss of dignity;
Loss of a sense of self;
Loss of trust;
Loss of confidence.

As Guidance Counsellors our priority is the student's welfare and providing continued support is essential, while ensuring that all guidelines are followed appropriately.

The Role of Schools: is to create an environment where individuals are not afraid to disclose abuse.

Final Thought:

The key to counselling a victim of sexual abuse is to facilitate regaining control. Language is central to this as it underpins understanding, acceptance and moving on.

Guidance on Dealing with Sexual Abuse...

FOR STUDENTS

Take the first step and tell someone you trust.
Take your time.
Know you are doing right by talking.
REMEMBER: You are not to blame.
REMEMBER: You did not invite it, it was forced upon you.
It will be tough but you can get through this.
Write a letter to the abuser that you can keep.
Make a list of the positive things about you.
Instead of saying 'I can't', say 'I can!'

FOR PARENTS

Take time to listen.
Show that you believe them.
Do not panic, stay calm.
Reassure them they were right to tell you.
Try not to question too much about what happened.
Seek advice to take the next step.

FOR THE PASTORAL TEAM

If abuse is disclosed to you, listen and be calm.
Reassure and do not promise confidentiality.
Remember the welfare of the student is the priority.
Follow the procedures outlined in the *Children First Guidelines*.
Inform the Designated Liaison Person in the school (Usually the Principal)
Document the information.
Take time for you.

Further Information...

Useful Websites

www.drcc.ie

The Dublin Rape Crisis Centre (DRCC) is a national organisation offering a wide range of services to those affected by rape, sexual assault, sexual harassment or childhood sexual abuse.
The services include: counselling, court accompaniment, training, and raising awareness.

The 24 Hour National Helpline: 1800 77 88 88

www.cari.ie

CARI is a voluntary organisation which provides support to children and families affected by sexual abuse.

www.sexualviolence.ie

This service provides free counselling and support to those who have suffered rape or child sexual abuse.

www.oneinfour.ie

One in Four is a registered charity offering practical support to men and women in dealing with the aftermath of sexual abuse.

Essential Reading

Children First: National Guidance for the Protection and Welfare of Children. Department of Children and Youth Affairs.

Child Protection Procedures for Primary and Post-Primary Schools Department of Education and Skills.

Chapter 8
Suicide

Snowdrop
The fragile snowdrop, on its own, is vulnerable. It finds strength and potential when it grows in clusters or company.

Suicide

Suicide – everyone's worst nightmare. So many of us have been touched by suicide, whether it is an uncle, an aunt, a brother, a sister, a parent, a cousin, a friend, it is devastating. The intense shock, numbness, sadness, disbelief and rejection is compounded by questions of why?

Why did I not see signs of despair?
Why did he not talk to me?
Why did she take her own life?

In recent years, I have worked with students as young as fourteen who have known and lost four or five friends to suicide in one year alone. It is an alarming situation for young people to try and come to terms with. The fact that more people die by suicide in Ireland today than in traffic accidents is both worrying and distressing. Why is there such an increase? Is it because there are more stresses in our lives with which some cannot cope? Have we become, ironically, more isolated and detached in this social media age? Is it because suicide is no longer seen as the taboo it was? It is difficult to know.

The reasons for suicide are complex. Sometimes, there are possible signs; sometimes there are not. There is no doubt that the person is in a very dark place and sees no other way out. In that moment, their only need is to get away from the terrifying and extreme emotions they are experiencing. They want an escape.

The accounts that follow highlight the confusion, anger, guilt and the grief that result in the aftermath of suicide.

A School's Response to Suicide

When a school community is devastated by suicide there are three main supports that the Principal can utilise:

1. The Students Themselves

When the atmosphere in a school is of overwhelming grief, the students often find resilience and strength in each other. They support each other. They look out for each other. They share their feelings openly and honestly. They stick together.

As teachers and managers, we can encourage this peer support. It is a critical element in helping young people feel that they belong and promotes a communal sense of togetherness rather than isolation. Specific rooms can be made available to the students to grieve. They should be given the freedom to step out of class and into a physical space where they can gather, talk and cry. Some might choose to continue attending class, needing the structure and normality it offers.

2. The School Community

It is vital that the management team tailor their own School Policy on Critical Incidents and set up a Critical Incident Team, which comprises the Principal, Deputy Principals, Year Heads, Guidance Counsellors and Chaplain. Any school which has not yet compiled this policy should make it a priority. Such planning and preparation is fundamental in the handling of critical incidents. Each member should be given specific tasks which ensure that as a school we respond appropriately for the welfare of the whole community. The following are just some of the formal procedures that might be put into action:

1.   Visiting the home of the bereaved by the Principal and School Chaplain is an important support that the school community can offer to the family;

2.   Bringing together the full staff to brief them on how to respond to the students and how to cope and manage their own feelings after such tragic news;

3.   Dividing the year group into smaller groups to write out how they are feeling at that moment, supported by two teachers per group;

4.   Organising a memorial evening in the school where students and family come together in song and prayer. A night-light can be lit by each person in memory of the student who has passed away;

5.   Participating in the funeral allows the school community to share in the grieving process with the family.

3. The Community Outside of the School.

Parents should be welcomed to the school to comfort their sons and daughters. The local priests may also arrive to offer assistance. The HSE and Department of Education Psychologists and counsellors will make contact to give advice. Principals and teachers from surrounding schools may phone to offer condolence and help. Everyone works together. Each community comes together to cope with this most traumatic event.

The Follow Up...

In the months that follow, the students, parents, teachers and management can prove how a community working together can support each individual following a trauma. In a practical way the events create a new focus on strengthening student resilience and self-confidence, encouraging more openness, dialogue and listening.

Use should be made of outside agencies who can be invited to talk to students and parents on a variety of issues including stress-management, coping-skills and study techniques. The Student Council can be encouraged to make suggestions beyond the boundaries of just the academic i.e. personal and social issues.

In all that is done, the aim is to put in place opportunities for students to talk and discuss and also to provide them, with the skills to cope with challenges in a healthy manner.

Introducing Brian... Aged 18...

Brian was in his final year in school when his uncle died by suicide. When he came to see me, he presented withdrawn, pale, in shock and in denial. He could not believe what had happened. There were no warning signs. His uncle seemed to have it all, a wife and family, a job and good health.

Brian was struggling to come to terms with the reality of his loss. He was overwhelmed by emotions. He could not sleep or eat, he was having panic attacks and he had lost all motivation for school. He felt he had lost a piece of himself.

The Approach I Used...

I needed to provide Brian with the opportunity and space to express the emotions that had been awakened in him by his uncle's suicide. In dealing with their own grief, his parents were unable to talk about it. He worried that his family was falling apart. He could not talk to his friends, as he feared he would be doing an injustice to his uncle's memory.

Over the next six weeks I set out to achieve a number of goals:

1. To listen and develop a trust.
2. To encourage Brian to talk about his uncle (using his name). In the initial stages of the counselling process, Brian spoke continuously. Students who have been bereaved usually demonstrate this desire for repetition. The student will constantly refer to the deceased, over and over, telling the same stories. It is this necessity to keep their memory alive that helps to fight feelings of fear and loss.
3. To help him understand that everyone grieves differently and that his parents also needed time.
4. To address the overwhelming questions of 'why?' It was important to allow Brian to ask, even though there were no answers.
5. To recognise each emotion he was feeling and put them into context, through talking and written exercises. Brian needed to name his feelings and to understand them. The act of writing allowed him to see, in black and white, how we can separate our thoughts from our feelings. One thought he wrote, for example: I think my family is falling apart. For the feeling, he wrote; I feel afraid.
6. To encourage him to tell his friends how he felt. They could offer him valuable peer support.
7. To refocus him on his own future goals and plans.

For the final appointment I asked Brian to write to his uncle and to say whatever came naturally to him. It was a task he found cathartic and worthwhile.

This is a letter he wrote in the weeks that followed:

We do not know why you left us so unexpectedly and we never will. We do not think of how you left us but how you were when you were with us. You were the quietest of all your family. You were adored by your wife and son, who miss you so much. We all miss you. You did have friends and a very loving family. I wish you knew this before. Everyone was devastated by your passing away.

Your son seems to be getting on ok, but I don't think he fully understands why you left us. I don't think your passing has hit him yet. Your wife appears to be coping but deep down I think she is devastated. They both miss you so much. She hasn't gone back to work yet, but I don't blame her. I heard her say how she will be ok for money because she will get the widow's pension. I found that very upsetting. She is a widow in her 40s!

Mom and dad are finding it hard too. Dad hasn't slept properly in weeks. I still can't believe that you are gone. Sometimes people say "Sorry to hear about your uncle". I say thanks and then question myself. What happened to my uncle? Did he die? Oh yes, he committed suicide. I find it hard to believe this has happened. You often hear about people committing suicide and feel bad for their family. But it's only when something like this hits your own family that you truly understand.

The only thing that is missing now is you. I hope you are happy now and at peace.

The Follow Up...

Brian found that by expressing his emotions through the spoken and written word he could make some sense of his grief. It could never bring his uncle back but it allowed him to understand what he was feeling. He did not feel so alone when he had a place to share his thoughts and worries. The six weeks of counselling prior to his Leaving Certificate gave him back some control of his own life. He understood that, even temporarily, he could now focus on his studies and the exams that lay ahead.

He went on to college the following year, where he attended the counselling service for a brief time. He continues to grieve for his uncle and still worries about his parents, aunt and cousin and how their lives have changed. His family has not fallen apart but it has been very much damaged. The strain of coping with his uncle's suicide has tested all relationships and changed the atmosphere in the home.

Brian made the first step in coping with the bereavement, by allowing others in. He used the supports that were available to him and gave him the courage to move forward.

The following contribution was written by Elma Walsh, Mother of Donal Walsh, the Kerry teenager who touched many lives while battling cancer:

"Donal's Livelife Foundation was set up by his family in order to bring forward his causes of providing age appropriate teenage facilities in hospital and hospice centres, aswell as promoting his anti-suicide message. #Livelife message." - donalwalshlivelife.org

Donal and his friends did and still do enjoy life and they have the normal teenage worries and stresses of girlfriends, clothes and the up-coming Leaving Cert and where they will be this time next year. But what keeps them grounded to my mind is firstly they all play a sport, they all talk freely about their feelings and worries, they are all good to each other and they all have some form of Spirituality in their lives that they are not shy about sharing.

The opportunities Donal had in life were the very same as any of your teenagers, a chance of a good education, being involved in local football and rugby teams, good friends, and even when he was first sick he used his illness to fundraise for Crumlin. I suppose with Donal he USED his opportunities. He used football and rugby to meet his heroes, he used his education to write his articles and articulate his feelings, he made the most of the life he had left with his friends and even when he knew the cancer was terminal, he used the media and the opportunity he was given by Brendan O'Connor to speak out about how important Life and Living it is. So what I am saying here is use the opportunities you are given.

We need to let children know from a very young age that it is ok to talk, talk about their feelings and not being afraid to say what is on their mind, it will help them. They shouldn't have to deal with these confusing and disorientating feelings / thoughts by themselves. By talking to someone a friend, a teacher, a parent, an aunt or uncle or phone one of the many organisations like Outreach, Console, Pieta House, they have open doors.

Donal's message was a simple one really, it was aimed at teenagers but when it went out others listened and took up the challenge too, it is to live your life, the life he knew he would not be able to live. Donal saw the great support and the good things he was leaving behind in life. The only negative he had for the last few months was leaving behind all these beautiful things. Donal fought for his life and to live it and he did, he made the most of every day he had. Here was a 16-year-old who could have given up very early on and stayed in bed all day and no one would blame him for it, but God gave Donal a challenge and he took it on.
Donal asked his peers to *Appreciate Life and to Live it.*

Elma Walsh
February 2014

Reflection...

When I set out to write this book my main objective was to let students know that they are never alone. There are always options to how we cope with stress in our lives and different ways to handle it. When we are feeling down we tend to listen to the voice in our own head saying negative things and encouraging negative behaviour. No matter how desperate or hopeless we feel, there are people we can turn to, who will listen to this voice and who can help.

Of all the chapters I have written, this has been the most difficult. I struggled with wanting to protect the memories of those who have died by suicide and with wanting to offer advice and support to those affected by their loss.

The question for all concerned in the aftermath of suicide is 'why?' This question causes further heartbreak and often guilt but can never be satisfactorily answered. Our focus as Guidance Counsellors, teachers and parents is to help others to live.

So what can we do to prevent suicide? There are a number of strategies that can be employed to create resilience, coping and higher self-esteem in young people. It is hoped that these strengths of character would support any individual contemplating suicide. There are three key approaches which can be used in schools to prevent the development of suicidal thoughts:

1. Promote and encourage coping strategies to handle stressful situations. Essentially this is personal to each individual and is determined by their own self-worth and self-esteem. It can be aided by involvement in extra-curricular activities or programmes such as:

The Resilience / Friends First Programme;
The *Meitheal* Programme;
The Buddy Programme;
The Amber Flag Initiative;
All of which, aim to encourage the development and growth of self-esteem in students.

2. To recognise and respond appropriately to students presenting with depression or self-harm, who may develop suicidal thoughts at a later stage.

3. To encourage that all communities, in and outside school are places where young people can ask, approach, talk and be heard. An open, respectful and listening – rich environment will be healthy and consequently facilitate better mental health.

Final Thought:

There is an old saying that "children should be seen and not heard". As educators and parents our role is to create an environment in which each child and young adult has a voice; a voice that is heard and is listened to. By encouraging this we are encouraging positive attitudes and consequently, positive mental health.

FOR STUDENTS

Talk to someone you trust.
Know that you can get through this, even though you might feel that you can't.
All the feelings you are experiencing are normal.
It's okay to be angry.
Take one day at a time.
If someone you know speaks of harming themselves, report it immediately.

FOR PARENTS

Allow yourself time to grieve.
Acknowledge all the feelings you are experiencing.
Talk to a family member or friend.
Allow yourself to be angry-it doesn't take away from still loving the person who died.
Write a letter to the person who died.
Make use of the support groups that are available in your area.
Look after yourself-chat with your doctor if you need to.

FOR THE PASTORAL TEAM

Implement *The Critical Incident Policy* and follow *The Guidelines for Mental Health Promotion and Suicide Prevention and Well-Being in Post-Primary Schools* (www.education.ie)
Make contact with the necessary agencies.
The National Office for Suicide Prevention (NOSP) runs an invaluable two-day in-service training course in suicide first aid, ASIST (Applied Suicide Intervention Skills Training).
Use the support structure of your colleagues.
Take time out when needed.
Acknowledge your own emotions.

Further Information...

Useful Websites

www.console.ie

Console is a National Organisation that offers support, counselling and helpline services to people in suicidal crisis and those bereaved by suicide.

Console Helpline: 1800 247 247
Text 'Help' to 51444

www.samaritans.ie

The **Samaritans** service is available 24 hours a day, to provide confidential support to those in despair and distress.

www.pieta.ie

Pieta House has nine centres around the country that provide a free, therapeutic approach to people in suicidal distress and also to those who engage in self-harm. Appointments can be made directly, without a referral from a doctor or a psychiatrist.

www.suicideaware.ie

Suicide Aware is a voluntary organisation that helps to bring awareness to the issues of depression and suicide. Their "Amber Flag Initiative" aims to encourage a cultural change within schools and societies towards the promotion of positive mental health. A growing number of schools have achieved the Amber Flag Award by actively promoting positive mental health.

www.1life.ie

1life is a 24 hour suicide prevention Helpline service, for anyone in suicidal distress.

1life 24 hour National Helpline: 1800 24 7 100

The Department of Education and Skills' publication, *Responding to Critical Incidents – Guidelines for Schools,* is an essential read for all school leaders and is available on www.education.ie.

Chapter 9
Young Parents

Apple Blossom
The youthful flower of the apple tree bears the fruit, and the cycle of its life continues.

Young Parents

My own school experience of teenage pregnancy falls in line with the national average. According to the Central Statistics Office (CSO), the number of teenagers giving birth in Ireland has fallen by 35% in the last decade. The decline in rates must be attributed to more open communication and information, relationship and sexuality education and changing attitudes towards underage sex.

All the students I worked with had already informed their parents before the news broke in school. So by that stage, the initial shock had passed and they were beginning to come to terms with the realisation that they were pregnant. In all the cases, the fathers of the unborn children were not known to me and I had no communication with them. Not all young fathers will have the emotional, financial or personal wherewithal to cope with fatherhood. The role of the Guidance Counsellor in this situation is to guide and lend assistance to the teenage mother. When a student is pregnant, her own welfare is of paramount importance. The age of the student and the circumstances around the pregnancy will determine the subsequent actions.

The young parent-to-be faces a bewildering mix of emotions:

Concern about going to the doctor and the hospital;
Fear of how they will cope as a parent;
Embarrassment at what others will think;
Worrying about school or college;
Concern about financial implications.

Through the counselling process I addressed these emotions and concentrated on two key issues:

1.   Looking into preparations for the birth of the baby;
2.   Coping with reactions of others towards them.

The Role of the Principal is to:

1.   Refer the matter to the HSE, if the student is under the age of 17. They in turn, contact the Gardaí, who will investigate the situation. In certain circumstances, a person who has sex under the age of 17, or, with someone else under the age of 17, may be prosecuted by the Gardaí;
2.   Make contact with the parents of the student;
3.   Ensure the student receives counselling and support in school;
4.   Liaise with the Guidance Counsellor if outside professional help is required.

Introducing Hannah.. Aged 17...

Wherever there was laughter to be heard in the school, Hannah was usually at the centre of it! She was a vivacious and happy student. Despite finding school difficult, she rarely missed a day. She loved the social aspect to school and was well liked by her peers and teachers. Hannah was referred to me by her Year Head when word broke that she was pregnant. She was happy to come and talk about it and to express her worries and concerns.

The Approach I Used...

Hannah's family and friends were already aware of her pregnancy and she was becoming accustomed to the notion that she was going to be a mother. She still needed reassurance and the time and space to voice her fears and concerns around the future and what it might hold.

She asked herself questions like:

Can I cope with a baby?
Should I finish school?
How can I afford to raise a child?

The counselling process allowed her to find answers to these questions. She was a capable girl with good self-esteem, a supportive boyfriend and a good family support structure, so I took a very practical approach to helping her.

I set up an appointment with the local Teen Parent Support Programme. This Programme is run in several locations around the country. It is a wonderful service for all young parents under the age of 20. It offers financial support, advice and practical information on childcare, social welfare and housing. It is also an excellent resource for parents of young parents who will have many questions to be answered.

With the support of her teachers and Year Head we devised a reduced timetable and extra help if needed, which encouraged her to continue her studies.

We discussed her future college options and taking a year out.

With the support of home, school and friends she no longer felt alone. Her confidence in her own capabilities improved as she prepared herself for the changes ahead.

Hannah's Story [written after the birth of her baby]:

The past two years have been pretty busy. I was the typical teenager. I loved going out with my friends, getting DVDs and watching movies and having a carefree life. I was just finished fifth year in school when I discovered I was pregnant, and at the beginning I didn't really believe it or take much notice. Two days later when I told one of my best friends, the reality started to settle in. I kept thinking, is this really happening to me or is it a dream? Why me? I could barely manage to do my homework on time. How could I be in charge of another person's life.

Telling my family was the hardest thing I ever had to do. Before I told them, all I could hear in my head was mom's voice saying, "You don't have to be great at school or exams but just do your best that's all you can do". My mom is the type of person who just wanted the best for me and to finish school, and after that she was happy. I prepared myself for the worst. I can remember sitting down and my mom looking at my face. All I said was "I'm so sorry I didn't mean to upset you". That was all I was worried about. After that, I lay on my bed looking at the ceiling thinking "This is it. My life is over. I can't take care of a baby I'm only 17".

Over the next few days my aunts and uncles came to talk to me and each and every one of them had nothing but nice things to say. They each told me if I was ever stuck for anything, if I needed help with school and whatever choice I made, they would be behind me all the way. I thought long and hard about what I should do and decided that I was going to keep the baby. I only had a part-time job and I wasn't finished school but I made the decision that I was going to finish school and be the best mom I could be.

I worked and saved as much money as I could. I returned to school in September thinking that I was going to be looked at differently and made fun of but I had such great friends who helped me with my school work and were there just to talk. The teachers in school were great and were really concerned about how I was doing and that I wasn't falling behind in work.

I had a scan and there it was, the confirmation that I had a baby growing in my tummy. I soon realised that every decision I made in the future would affect the baby. There was a lot of preparation before Christmas as I was due in February and had to get my work handed in before the exams. Before my due date, the nurse told me that the baby was ready to arrive. My heart sank. I got butterflies in my tummy. I had to go home, get my bags and go back to the hospital. The next night there it was, in my arms. The little boy I had been waiting for. Now everything I did in life was all for this baby.

I don't want anyone reading this to think for one minute that I was great at school or that I found it easy having a baby. It's not easy. It's the hardest job in the world being a mum, making decisions, doing night feeds, always running around the place, but is the most rewarding job in the world.

I finished my Leaving Cert and took a year out. I went to college for a year, which I loved, as the course was especially equipped for people with children so everyone in the group understands your situation so you don't feel alone. My son started preschool and I work part time and live in my own house. Life couldn't get any better for me. I have everything I could ever want.

For those of you who are mums to be, keep your head up, keep smiling and know that one day your baby will be proud of you for the effort and hard work you put in. Whether you live at home or with a friend or family member, remember things take time and if you want them to work you must work at them.

The Follow Up...

The year after the birth of her son, Hannah completed an Applied Computer Training Course in a local College of Further Education. It is a course specifically designed for young parents and provides childcare assistance and a weekly attendance allowance. This type of course is unique to Further Education Colleges and is not offered by Universities or Institutes of Technology.

Hannah has since secured employment and now lives with her partner, the father of her baby. They have always had a very healthy and supportive relationship. She has shown herself to be a competent and loving mother. She embraced the role positively and has built a home that is happy and functional. Several factors contributed to aiding Hannah's transition from teenager to young parent:

Her long-term relationship;
Her boyfriend was emotionally mature and in full time employment;
She completed her Leaving Certificate;
Her family's response was both supportive and practical.

Introducing Alison... Aged 15...

Alison was a good student with an impeccable attendance record and a close group of friends. However, in her fifth year, I do recall noticing a change in her demeanour. She was withdrawn, tired and appeared sad. This image however, was not an uncommon expression among her peers. It was late January when her mother contacted the school and met with myself and Alison's Year Head. She informed us that Alison was now six months pregnant! In a sea of uniforms, her baggy jumper had hidden her secret well. It was her face that perhaps told the true story.

The Approach I Used...

I explained to Alison's mother that I would be informing the Principal of her pregnancy. As the Designated Liaison Person for Child Protection, she was obliged to contact the HSE to inform them, as Alison was underage. The situation would then be investigated in conjunction with the Gardaí. They could prosecute for an offence called 'defilement', which in simple terms means having sex with somebody under the age of 17.

It was also necessary at this point to make all her teachers aware, so that they could offer her any support needed.

Alison's parents had scarcely three months to come to terms with the pregnancy and prepare for the changes ahead. They still had younger children in the house to feed, clothe and care for. Not only did they worry about Alison's health and ability to cope, but they worried about their own capacity to cope financially, physically and emotionally.

Alison's relationship with the father of baby was also unstable and volatile and added to the already stressful situation. He had no interest in a relationship with her and did not take any responsibility for the consequences of his actions.

My immediate role was to offer a listening ear and practical support. During the next two months Alison spoke of the reaction by other students to her pregnancy, the name calling and the stares. She felt publically humiliated by the taunts and exclusion. At 15, some of Alison's peers reacted negatively and ridiculed her because she was different. She stood out from the crowd and was bullied because of this. Older students, at 16 or 17 are usually more supportive and understanding. As her counsellor, I concentrated on building her confidence and self-belief, by encouraging her to focus on what she could do rather than on what she could not. At only fifteen, she faced numerous challenges. Her body was changing and her emotions intensified. Her life was about to alter considerably. Preparing for the baby's arrival became a necessary distraction for her.

Alison's Story [written after the birth of her son]:

Finding out I was 15 and pregnant was the scariest thing I ever experienced. I wasn't even the type of girl who went around 'meeting' people. I had a very strong, bubbly personality and plenty of friends. But when it came to fellas I was always shy.

Then I met a fella who was 18 years old. Being 15, you think you know everything. Honestly, I did fall head over heels for him. It came to the day that we slept together. Not long after that he was with a new girl. I didn't feel well for weeks but kept putting off getting a test done. I had no morning sickness and kept telling myself I couldn't be pregnant.

The day I finally took the test I felt absolutely sick before taking it. My heart was beating rapidly. I couldn't even breathe. My head was doing ninety! At that moment I felt so alone. I was pregnant! I told the father of the baby and he said it wasn't his. He totally ignored me for the first few months. I kept thinking it would all be over in a couple of weeks. Believe me I did get very low.

I wrote a letter, just for me, explaining how I felt, how alone, heartbroken and miserable, thinking nothing else could be done. At this stage I didn't even realise how serious it was keeping this to myself, the complication of being pregnant. I decided not to tell my family as it was Christmas. I was now six months pregnant. I was able to hide my bump because it was winter and I always wore baggy jumpers.

After Christmas I eventually told my parents. No one in my family would even speak to me. They were so hurt they wouldn't even look at me. The Gardai were called because I was underage. When everyone in school found out I was called every name under the sun. The rumours started. They got worse and worse by the day. Despite the horrible things that were said, I showed up every day and sat through it. People can really leave you feeling so alone and not even knowing the true story.

I stopped contact with the baby's father when he became obsessive. Even though he said nasty things about me, he kept calling me and telling me what to do. I finished in school when I was eight months pregnant. I stopped going out. I did get massive - but just my bump! I was eventually induced because I was ten days over my due date. After hours of labour I had a beautiful baby boy who I love to bits. After three days I was allowed to return home.

I came back to school and was greatly helped by my Guidance Counsellor and my Year Head. I kept my head down. I found it very hard being separated from my baby but kept it together. My mother and my son developed a strong bond and I found that, at times, very hard to deal with.

But as low as you might feel, you can always get through it. I went from being 15 and pregnant, to being a mum. Now I'm a single mum, doing my Leaving Cert with support from my family.

I will never be able to thank the people who helped me so much. So if anyone was to take anything from me writing this, it is to tell your parents and go to a doctor. As much as they might be angry at first, they can help.

The Follow Up...

Alison really struggled that final year in school. The relationship with her ex-boyfriend and the difficulties around maintenance and access all took its toll on the family. It was not an easy year. The Principal and I met with her parents on several occasions to offer support and advice on how to cope. They too needed someone to talk to and somewhere to express their shock and concern. We arranged a meeting with the Garda Liaison Officer who was extremely helpful, supportive and sensitive to the circumstances. They were also very well supported by the Teen Parent Support Programme.

Alison was forced to grow up quickly. Her life changed radically. Gone were the days of going out with friends, chatting about boys and having fun. She was now a mum, trying to balance looking after her son with completing her Leaving Certificate. She had to deal with motherhood, an estranged partner, study, stress, anxiety and the legal challenges around maintenance and access.

She secured her place in a College of Further Education. The college organised child care for her son so that she could attend her course knowing that he was cared for. She has come a long way from the innocent 15-year-old, who did not have a care in the world. She is now a loving, caring and competent young mother, with a family to support her.

Introducing Jessica... Aged 17...

Jessica was a quiet and mannerly student. As her Guidance Counsellor I had met with her on a few occasions to discuss her plans and options after the Leaving Certificate. She had always spoken about training to be a beautician, a career I felt she would be well suited to. She did not need much guidance, she had it all planned out and was well organised. She applied for several courses to keep her options open. She was ready for the next phase of her life, or so I thought! Not long after the exams finished, I heard that Jessica was pregnant.

I was well aware of the changes this would bring to her life and knew that all her plans would now be put on hold. The one thing that would get her through the next few months was the support of her family and her long term boyfriend. She had to adjust to the realisation that she was soon to be a mother. As her classmates celebrated their graduation ball that September, Jessica was learning to cope with a new baby and all the responsibilities it brings.

The Approach I Used...

Jessica had finished her Leaving Certificate before the news broke of her pregnancy. The part I played was to direct her to the supports offered outside of school and to offer any advice in the near future. These supports included:

An appointment with the Teen Parents Support Service to advise on financial and practical issues;

A referral to the college admissions office she had applied to, to explain her option to defer her place.

Her family had it all under control. Her stable and long-term relationship was a beneficial factor in determining how Jessica managed.

Jessica's Story... Her Secret

It was my final year of school. I was extremely nervous about sitting my Leaving Cert exams. In March of that year, I found out I was pregnant. I was so shocked and terrified. The Leaving Cert had been the only thing on my mind, now it was the last thing I thought about. I didn't tell my Mum until after the Leaving Cert in June. At that stage I was already five and a half months pregnant. I couldn't hide it any more. I had been too embarrassed to tell anyone. I didn't want to have to deal with all the looks I would get and the whispering that would continue every day.

I was with my boyfriend for three years. He was a huge support throughout the pregnancy and he got me through every minute of it. It was the hardest year of my life.

A year later, I am still with my boyfriend. He has a job and we have our own house and a beautiful and healthy baby girl. In September I will be going into my first year of college and I'm so looking forward to it. I have always wanted to be a beautician and now I can follow my dream. I will be doing a Diploma in Beauty Therapy. I'm very lucky that my Mum will take care of my baby daughter so that I can attend college and get my qualification. She has also been a great support to me.

The Follow Up...

Jessica has been very fortunate to have so much support around her, especially that of her boyfriend. To fulfil her dream of becoming a beautician will make a huge difference to her own life and the life of her daughter. It will give her back the confidence she lost and replace any feelings of embarrassment or disappointment with pride and fulfilment. She will continue to make sacrifices and choices about her child's welfare just as any mother does.

Motherhood is daunting, especially during the teenage years. Jessica's stable family structure, healthy relationship and the prospect of a career, all made the transition to this adult world smoother. Their new family unit was strong, functional and positive.

Reflection...

Being a teenage parent is not an easy job. The initial fear and panic, the embarrassment and worry are compounded by the fact that each young mother is still going through change and development herself.

For parents of teenage mothers and fathers, it is also hugely stressful. They are at a stage when they have almost reared their own family and suddenly they are thrown into a world of new responsibilities. Teenage pregnancies are unplanned. Teenagers do not have the life experience or emotional development to understand the implications of parenthood. Essentially, grandparents must make the choices and decisions for the future.

Young fathers must also offer emotional and practical supports and are faced with a variety of obligations. They need to realise that having a baby is for life. They need to understand that they are now responsible for another life and may have to pay maintenance of up to €120 a week per child, for as long as their children are in full time education. This amount can change depending on the father's circumstances.

Being a young parent is no longer the taboo it was and the services that are now available are excellent. The websites are very informative and the help and advice given by all the agencies is extremely useful.

The Role of the School...

Is to continue to raise awareness of how teenagers can protect themselves sexually, emotionally and physically through Relationship and Sexuality Education. Where they understand the consequences of unprotected sex and where they can learn how to say 'No'.

The Role of the Parents...

Is to have open communication to help their son / daughter to make healthy decisions on sex and relationships.

The parents' page on www.b4udecide.ie offers very valuable advice and sex education information for parents.

- An unmarried mother has automatic and full rights of guardianship and custody of her child.

- An unmarried father has no automatic rights to his child. He has a right to apply for access, custody and guardianship.

- A father does not get guardianship rights as a result of his name being on the birth certificate of his child.

- Both parents have a responsibility to maintain their child.

- It is generally good for children to be in touch with both parents.

- Having the father's name on the birth cert does not mean that the mother will not get One Parent Family Payment.

The above information was made available by 'Treoir', the National Information Centre for Unmarried Parents. (2012)

Final Thought:

In responding to crisis issues, it is important to have details of local support services readily available. Having a Contacts List is essential to providing immediate and appropriate care.

FOR STUDENTS

If you think you might be pregnant it is very important that you tell someone.
Go to your GP, as soon as possible to get checked out.
Take time to get used to the idea of being pregnant.
Avail of all the agency support around you.
Don't give up on your own goals and what you want to achieve.

FOR PARENTS

Take time to adjust to finding out you are to be a grandparent.
Get support from family and friends.
Research the help and advice available.
Continue to communicate with your son / daughter.
Devise a plan for after the child is born.

FOR THE PASTORAL TEAM

Remain calm.
Explore if parents / guardians know of the pregnancy.
If the student is under the age of consent, *Child Protection Guidelines* must be followed.
Check with the student how they are physically and emotionally.
Where it is necessary to inform a parent or the principal, discuss the process sensitively.
Let the student know about the services available to her / him.
Let the student know she is not on her own.

Useful Websites

www.teenparents.ie

Run by the **Teen Parent Support Programme,** this website offers invaluable information and advice to both young parents and grandparents, during all stages of pregnancy.

www.cura.ie

Crisis Pregnancy Support Service offers:

- Support and counselling for young parents;
- A free CURA School Awareness Programme for 2nd year students onwards;
- Support for grandparents.

CURA Helpline: 1850 622 626

www.crisispregnancy.ie

The HSE Crisis Pregnancy Programme provides education, information and resources to schools, parents and young people. It offers a number of publications to assist teachers in providing sex education to young people. It also is responsible for funding other organisations which offer counselling.

www.treoir.ie

Treoir (the Irish word for guidance) is the national federation of services for unmarried parents and their children. It provides information and advice and has produced a wide range of publications on relevant issues.

Treoir Helpline: 1890 252 084
Email: *info@treoir.ie*

Useful Reading:

Key Contact – Responding to Crisis Pregnancy – Information and Service Directory for Community and Health Professionals.

Produced by the HSE with the support of the Crisis Pregnancy Agency.

A Note Under The Door

A note under the door
Was all it took
To begin a journey
Of healing
Though the road is bumpy
I've come to learn
I'm never alone.
A feeling once so hopeless
Has been transformed
And I see a new light
It is always welcoming
And always there
Even when times get tough
I know I will pull through
Talking is still hard
But I know it is for the best
I can open up in here
And show myself honestly
The wall I've spent so long building up
Is slowly crumbling down
And I see a new me start to emerge.

Written by Elizabeth
Aged 18

These poetic lines capture the courage of all students taking the first step in counselling. It is never easy and often takes many attempts, but it is rewarding.

To school leaders, your understanding and awareness of the issues confronting young people today will assist the promotion of policies and procedures on student welfare.

To parents, look for the support and resources that are available to you. The strength and courage you show will help your son or daughter to develop positive and healthy coping skills.

To students, take the step to speak out and let your voice be heard. I hope, like Elizabeth, you find the door is always open and realise you are never alone.

Acknowledgements

Thank you to all the students I have worked with, who taught me to be patient and resilient. You are my best teachers. To their parents and guardians who believed in them and the power of talking.

Thank you to Cathal, who has accompanied me on this journey of writing and rewriting and gave continuously of his love and support. His love of the written word and dedication to teaching and learning has been inspirational. Without his encouragement these stories would have remained silently in my filing cabinet.

Thank you to my parents, John and Ann – the 'Wonder Counsellors' who instilled in me a desire to help others and not to give up.

Thank you to my sisters, Ruth and Grace and my brothers, Peter, Dermot and Colm, for guiding me on the way.

Thank you to my editor and 'critical friend' Derek West. He gave generously of his time and his rigorous and creative editorial skills. His wisdom and insight are to be found between, and in, these pages.

A special thank you to my co-designer Ailish Murphy for giving endlessly of her time, her talents and her technological wisdom. Thank you for your dependability and huge input into the design and layout of The Guided Way. Thank you for your friendship and for "counselling the counsellor" over many cups of tea!

Thank you to Shay Bannon for his enthusiasm and for being pro-active in getting The Guided Way directly to the Principals and Deputy Principals and into the heart of our school communities.

Thank you to Clive Byrne and the NAPD for their support and endorsement and for seeing the potential and benefit of The Guided Way as useful and necessary reading for all school leaders.

Thank you to Pat Kinsella, for giving me the opportunity to develop my role as a Guidance Counsellor and for having faith in me.

Thank you to Michelle Sliney, Cáit Breathnach, Maria O'Sullivan and Daithí O'Gallachóir for always being open to another way.

Thank you to my colleagues in Coláiste Choilm, especially the Guidance team of Sephine Hallahan, Áine Higgins and Chaplain Fr. James McSweeney, for your friendship and encouragement.

Thank you to the Year Heads, tutors and teachers of Coláiste Choilm who, on the frontline, show skill and intuition beyond their training.

Thank you to the wider staff who shape the atmosphere and physical environment to produce a school so conducive to learning and positive interaction.

Thank you to my friend and colleague, the gifted artist Niamh O'Neill, whose beautiful illustrations capture and express the sentiment behind the flower theme.

Thank you to Colum Layton who inspired me to be the counsellor I wanted to be.

Thank you to my supervisor, Tony Hegarty, for his enlightened insights into the world of human behaviour and psychotherapy.

Thank you to my fellow Guidance Counsellors who fight the restrictions of time and pressure to provide a valuable and dedicated service.

Thank you to the Cork Branch of The Institute of Guidance Counsellors for their support and endorsement of the book.

Thank you to Monika Stanczak and Tomek Majerski at Printout for their professionalism, reliability and positive approach.

Thank you to all the agencies and professionals to whom I have made referrals, especially the local doctors, mental health services, counsellors and the Gardaí.

Finally, a very sincere and heartfelt thanks to those who intervened with advice, direction and encouragement at different steps along *The Guided Way.*

A Word about the Author...

Lucy McCullen is a native of County Meath. She has been a Guidance Counsellor in Coláiste Choilm, Ballincollig, County Cork for the past twenty years. She completed a Masters in Guidance Counselling in 2013.

This book is the culmination of 20 years experience working with both teenagers and adults, offering support and advice to those faced with a variety of challenges.

Notes:

Notes: